D0602547

sewing modkid style

sewing **modkid** style

modern threads for the cool girl

BY PATTY YOUNG

WILEY

John Wiley & Sons, Inc.

SENIOR EDITOR
Roxane Cerda

COPY EDITOR
Marylouise Wiack

SENIOR PROJECT EDITOR
Donna Wright

EDITORIAL MANAGER
Christina Stambaugh

VICE PRESIDENT AND PUBLISHER
Cindy Kitchel

VICE PRESIDENT AND EXECUTIVE PUBLISHER
Kathy Nebenhaus

ART DIRECTOR AND BOOK DESIGN
Tai Blanche

PHOTOGRAPHY
Patty Young
Dawn Bergeron

PATTERN TESTERS
Long ladies (Kristie, Apphia, Achaia, Abigail, and Abiah)
marie-madeline studio

Angela Condon
noisynorastore.etsy.com

Claire and Jessica
thegirlsingrey.com

Copyright © 2012 by John Wiley & Sons, Inc., Hoboken, New Jersey. All rights reserved.

Published by John Wiley & Sons, Inc., Hoboken, New Jersey

Published simultaneously in Canada

No part of this publication may be reproduced, stored in a retrieval system or transmitted in any form or by any means, electronic, mechanical, photocopying, recording, scanning or otherwise, except as permitted under Sections 107 or 108 of the 1976 United States Copyright Act, without either the prior written permission of the Publisher, or authorization through payment of the appropriate per-copy fee to the Copyright Clearance Center, 222 Rosewood Drive, Danvers, MA 01923, (978) 750-8400, fax (978) 646-8600, or on the web at www.copyright.com. Requests to the Publisher for permission should be addressed to the Permissions Department, John Wiley & Sons, Inc., 111 River Street, Hoboken, NJ 07030, (201) 748-6011, fax (201) 748-6008, or online at http://www.wiley.com/go/permissions.

Limit of Liability/Disclaimer of Warranty: The publisher and the author make no representations or warranties with respect to the accuracy or completeness of the contents of this work and specifically disclaim all warranties, including without limitation warranties of fitness for a particular purpose. No warranty may be created or extended by sales or promotional materials. The advice and strategies contained herein may not be suitable for every situation. This work is sold with the understanding that the publisher is not engaged in rendering legal, accounting, or other professional services. Before beginning any project, review the instructions carefully. If any doubts or questions exist, the services of a competent professional person should be sought. Always read and observe the safety precautions provided by the manufacturers of any tools, equipment, or supplies, and follow all accepted safety procedures. Because codes and regulations vary greatly, you always should check with authorities to ensure that your project complies with all applicable local codes and regulations. Due to differing conditions, tools, and individual skills, neither the publisher nor the author shall be liable for any damages, injuries suffered, or losses incurred as a result of following the information published in this work. The fact that an organization or Website is referred to in this work as a citation and/or a potential source of further information does not mean that the author or the publisher endorses the information the organization or Website may provide or recommendations it may make. Further, readers should be aware that Internet Websites listed in this work may have changed or disappeared between when this work was written and when it is read. Neither the publisher nor the author shall be liable for damages arising here from.

Trademarks: Wiley, the Wiley logo, and related trademarks are trademarks or registered trademarks of John Wiley & Sons, Inc. and/or its affiliates. "Modkid" and "Modern Threads for the Cool Girl" are trademarks owned by MODKID LLC. All other trademarks are the property of their respective owners. John Wiley & Sons, Inc., is not associated with any product or vendor mentioned in this book.

For general information on our other products and services or to obtain technical support please contact our Customer Care Department within the U.S. at (877) 762-2974, outside the U.S. at (317) 572-3993 or fax (317) 572-4002.

John Wiley & Sons, Inc., also publishes its books in a variety of electronic formats and by print-on-demand. Not all content that is available in standard print versions of this book may appear or be packaged in all book formats. If you have purchased a version of this book that did not include media that is referenced by or accompanies a standard print version, you may request this media by visiting http://booksupport.wiley.com. For more information about Wiley products, visit us at www.wiley.com.

Library of Congress Control Number: 2011941341

ISBN: 978-0-470-94768-5 (cloth)

Printed in China

10 9 8 7 6 5 4 3 2 1

Book production by John Wiley & Sons, Inc., Composition Services

Patty Young's original patterns are intended for non-commercial, personal use only and not to be used in the production of goods for sale in any quantity.

I would like to dedicate this book to my two princesses, Sophie and Sydney. Everything I do, I do for you.

Acknowledgments

Words cannot even begin to describe the amount of love and appreciation I have for my dear husband, Jon, who pretty much took over and ran the household (and very well done, I might add) from the moment I signed my book contract. Jon not only gave me all the space and time I asked for, but also all the moral support and encouragement I never asked for but so desperately needed.

A million and one thanks to my lovely studio assistants, Emalee Grambo and Emily Parks (a.k.a. Em & Em), for being my second pair of hands throughout this entire project. No kidding: they not only sewed about 99 percent of the samples that appear on these pages, but their actual *hands* are in all of the how-to photos. I couldn't have done all this without their help and positive disposition.

A huge thanks to my dear friend Dawn Bergeron, of Dawn Bergeron Photography, for assisting me with some of the photography in this book. Her group shots at the grungy alley and Funks Grove were breathtaking, and the connections she helped me make with the models' moms are absolutely priceless.

Hugs and kisses to my gorgeous little models—always eager, willing, and able—Sophie, Sydney, Anna, Maddie, Emersyn, Simone, and Giselle. Their sweet, smiling faces are the reason I do what I do! And, of course, a huge thanks to their moms, Dawn, Nikki, Dana, and Memuna, for their patience and flexibility!

The generous contributions made by the following suppliers made it possible for me to showcase a wide variety of fabrics, trims, and tools in this book. Thanks a bunch to the entire team at *Michael Miller Fabrics*, especially to Kathy Miller and Christine Osmers, for the endless supply of knit fabrics to play with and, of course, for their support and encouragement through all the crazy times. To Kelly Laws, of *Tacony Corporation*, for my wonderful Baby Lock Symphony sewing machine. To Caroline Geraci, of *The Fabric Fairy*, for supplying many of the funky imported knits and yummy organic velours you see throughout this book. To Tira Schulteis of *Brewer Distributors* and Tammi Hensley of *Prym-Dritz Corporation* for all the elastic and stretch trims I could ever wish for. And to Tracy Whitlock, of *Fairfield*, for the huge box of pillow forms and quilt battings.

I would like to extend a super-big thank you to Roxane Cerda at *Wiley Publishing* for believing in me and always being my biggest cheerleader. Because of her I can finally add "author" to my credentials. The entire team at *Wiley* was an absolute dream to work with.

Last but certainly not least, to my faithful blog readers, Twitter followers, and Facebook fans, I just want to say, "Thanks" and "You guys rock!" for making me feel the love, support, and excitement in all your comments. I hope you love it!

table of contents

Introduction

Times have certainly changed. Gone are the days of June Cleaver and Betty Draper when moms and kids alike were impeccably polished and dressed to the nines, every lock of hair perfectly in place at all times.

Nowadays, in this electronic and media-dominated culture of the twenty-first century, kids have a busier social life than we did. When my kids aren't mashing video game buttons while glued to the TV screen, they're being carted to swim lessons, gymnastics, dance class, birthday parties, school concerts, festivals, or sleepovers. And on the off chance that none of those activities are taking place at that moment, we're grocery shopping, running to the post office, or picking up Thai take-out. Never a dull moment. It's a "GO, GO, GO!" life.

Dressing the Modern, Active Child

When I set out to create the perfect MODKID wardrobe, I wanted to design clothes that kids actually *want t*o wear, not the idealistic version some parents have of what a kid *should* wear. Yes, those perfectly dressed, always poised kids who never run and never get dirty. I thought to myself, "What would make a kid actually *want* to reach for that item in the closet and put it on?" Busy lifestyles lead to individuality and a heightened sense of independence, thus even the youngest of kids want to dress themselves, pick out their own clothes, and act like "big kids."

The MODKID style is a perfect balance of . . .

- **Comfort.** No kid wants to run around town in a tight, stiff, overstuffed outfit. An active lifestyle demands clothes that move, run, jump, and bend with you. Enter . . . knits! And because knit fabrics stretch and contract to conform to their bodies, these garments can be easily pulled on even by the youngest in your household. All the designs in this book are made without zippers, buttons, snaps, or any other pesky closure too intricate for little fingers to handle.

- **Style.** No kid of mine should be caught wearing boring clothes. They're only kids once, so why not let them express their personalities in the items they wear? In this book you'll see that style and comfort *do* go hand in hand. All projects are designed so kids can help mix and match fabric prints to create a style of their own—a dash of whimsy here, a sprinkle of attitude there, just like her!

Why Knits?

Knitwear has been around much longer than you think and encompasses much more than just tracksuits and sweatshirts. Way back in 1916, fashion diva *Coco Chanel* became the icon for the liberated woman by using jersey in her hugely influential women's suits. Later, French designer *Sonia Rykiel*, who was crowned

Patty with her muses, from left to right, Maddie, Emersyn, Sydney, and Sophie.

"Queen of Knits" in the United States, was voted one of the world's 10 most elegant women in 1980. She proved that knitwear can follow any trend, and was the first designer to introduce inside-out seams and raw hems in her knit garments.

Of course, like anything else, knitwear went through its own "dark ages." The hideous polyester jumpsuits and men's leisure suits of the 1970s were to blame for the downfall of knits. Polyester soon became the icon for "bad taste," and along with it knits developed a stigma of their own.

In the decades that followed, knits virtually disappeared from consumer fabric stores, and most sewists deemed them as "scary to sew with." When I started sewing children's garments for profit in the mid 2000s, I was dying to try some of the German sewing patterns that were all the rage at the time, but a lot of them called for stretch fabrics. I realized then that I had only two choices: shop online for super-expensive imported knits—mostly from European brands like Marimekko (Finland) or Stenzo (the Netherlands), at prices upwards of $18 and $20 per yard (gulp)—or go to my local big box fabric store and buy cheap knits in boring solid colors that would compromise the quality of my clothing designs (double gulp). Well, being a sucker for cute prints—and good quality fabrics—I opted for the former and my profit margin suffered as a result, but hey, I made really cute clothes that lasted forever.

A couple of years later, when I received my fabric design contract from Michael Miller Fabrics, the first thing I said was, "Can we do these on knits?" Yes, I was still traumatized by the outrageous price I had been paying for knits, but since my kids practically live in comfy tees, twirly skirts, and leggings, it just seemed like the perfect medium for my designs. With a mixture of excitement and trepidation, we announced the release of our knits in April of 2010—a 27-piece collection printed on 100 percent cotton interlock . . . the softest, yummiest knits I had laid my eyes (and fingers) on! The excitement among sewing enthusiasts was truly palpable. I guess I wasn't the only one who was craving cute, quality, designer knits at affordable prices. When we went to Spring Quilt Market to showcase our knits, we stood back amazed as a constant stream of happy, smiling shop owners thanked us for "bringing knits back." The market was finally ready—*hurray!*

In the past couple of years, I have noticed a resurgence in knits, not only in the designer fabrics produced, but also in sewing patterns, tutorials, and blog posts in the marketplace. Knits are certainly back, and they're here to stay! And it's no surprise to me, especially when it comes to children's clothing. Knits are softer, warmer, and more comfortable than their woven counterparts. Garments sewn with knits can look as casual and simple or as stylish and sophisticated as you make them. And since knits don't wrinkle or ravel in the wash, they can save you tons of time (. . . all busy moms know the value of that!).

As Sir Francis Bacon once said, "Knowledge is Power," so let me arm you with the information you need to finally tackle that stack of beautiful, soft knits.

Getting Knitpicky: Types of Knit Fabrics

Knit fabric types are like ice cream flavors—too many to count. But just like ice cream flavors, they're all great in their own way! They range from very lightweight and almost sheer mesh to super-thick and plush stretch velours and fleeces. There are loose knits and tight knits, knits with two-way stretch, and knits with four-way stretch. I could get über-technical on you and delve into how the fabrics are manufactured, the history of each, and what-not, but in reality, in order to decide which types of fabric you'll use for each project, you only need to know a few important things.

- **Stretch.** How much does the fabric stretch and what is its recovery factor, meaning, how well does it bounce back after being stretched to the max? This will be especially important to know when sewing anything that will be worn over the knees or the elbows, so you don't end up with lumpy and bumpy garments.

- **Weight.** What is the thickness of the fabric, and does it have a visible texture or not? This will generally translate into drape as well . . .: thinner knits will hug your body and move with ease, while the thicker ones will hold their own shape better.

- **Fiber content.** Is it a natural fiber, like cotton, or a synthetic blend, like poly/cotton, or a purely synthetic fabric like nylon/Lycra or poly/rayon? As you'll see, there is a use and a need for each type.

- **Stability.** Do the edges lay flat or do they curl up when cut? Stable fabrics are easier to sew but those curled edges can add a grungy, funky look to T-shirt hems and sleeves when left unfinished.

So, let's get down to the nitty-gritty. In the next few pages I describe the most popular types of knit fabrics based on these four criteria, and then I give you examples of the best uses for each fabric based on the projects in this book.

Knit fabrics display at Waechter's Fine Fabrics, Asheville, North Carolina (www.waechters.com).

Always pre-shrink all your fabrics (wash, dry, and iron) before beginning any sewing project. Knit fabrics shrink more than woven fabrics so this step is a must for garment construction.

Interlock

- **Stretch.** Depending on the manufacturer, interlocks can stretch anywhere from 25 to 40 percent across the grain. They have a fair, but not exceptional, amount of recovery so they are more suitable for loose-fitting garments like T-shirts, dresses, skirts, and sleepwear.

- **Weight.** Interlock is a light- to medium-weight fabric with a fine rib on both sides.

- **Fiber content.** Most interlocks are 100-percent cotton, which translates into a softer, combed cotton feel but also means that they have a higher shrinkage factor than synthetic blends.

- **Stability.** Cotton interlocks are very stable. The cut ends lay flat and don't run. They're also super easy to sew and virtually wrinkle-free.

Cotton or cotton-blend interlocks can be used for all the projects in this book except the *Swimsuit* (page 136).

Jersey

- **Stretch.** Depending on the manufacturer, jerseys can stretch anywhere from 20 to 25 percent across the grain. They have a fair amount of recovery so they're suitable for T-shirts, dresses, pull-on pants, shorts, skirts, and sleepwear.

- **Weight.** Jersey is a light- to medium-weight fabric with a definite right and wrong side. There are thin vertical ribs on the right side (face) and wavy horizontal lines, or purls, on the wrong side (back).

- **Fiber content.** Fiber content can vary from cotton blends to synthetic blends.

- **Stability.** Jerseys are "unstable." The edges will curl when cut and can even run from the cut edge. Jerseys are not as thick as interlocks and not as warm. They are also clingier than interlocks,

Our sweet Harlequin Quilt is perfect to take on picnics and family outings.

which makes them perfect for casual dresses and lightweight skirts.

Jerseys can be used for all projects in this book except the *Swimsuit* (page 136).

Rib Knit

- **Stretch.** Rib knits, also commonly referred to as *ribbing,* have approximately 100 percent crosswise stretch. This stretch makes them perfect for neck bands, waistbands, and cuffs, but also suitable for leggings, T-shirts, and loungewear.

- **Weight.** Rib knits are medium- to heavy-weight fabrics with prominent vertical ribs on both the face and the back.

- **Fiber content.** Fiber content can vary from cotton blends to synthetic blends.

- **Stability.** Rib knits are highly stable. The edges will lay flat when cut. This makes them easy to sew and care for since they won't wrinkle.

Because of their great stability and recovery factor, rib knits are perfect to use for the top and bottom bands on the *Banded Tank Top* (page 86), for the cuffs on the *Leg Warmers* (page 46), and for the yoga waistbands on the *Yoga Pants* (page 58) and *A-Line Gored Skirt* (page 80). Rib knits are also ideal to use for the neck band and sleeve bands on the *Not-So-Plain Tee* (page 102), *Mondrian Shirt* (page 97), *Contrast V-Neck Sweater* (page 108), and *Bloom Dress* (page 129).

Double Knits

- **Stretch.** Double knit fabrics, like the ever-so-popular *Ponte di Roma*, have very minimal stretch and resist wrinkles better than any other knit fabric.

- **Weight.** Double knit is a firm, medium- to heavy-weight fabric that has fine ribs and usually looks the same on both sides.

- **Fiber content.** Fiber content can vary from cotton blends to synthetic blends.

- **Stability.** Double knits are very stable. The edges lay flat when cut. This makes them easy to sew and care for since they won't wrinkle.

Double knits would work beautifully for the *Not-So-Plain Tee* (page 102), *Bloom Dress* (page 129), and *Contrast V-Neck Sweater* (page 108). Avoid using double knits for projects that require *shirring* (two or more rows of elastic gathers), like the *Shirrley Tank Dress* (page 122), or a lot of gathering, like the *Twirly Tiered Skirt* (page 64), *Bubble Skirt* (page 69), or *Banded Tank Top* (page 86), because the extra thickness of this fabric would make it difficult to shirr or gather and would make for a very bulky and heavy piece.

Lycra (Spandex) and Lycra-Blends

- **Stretch.** Lycra, a trade name for spandex, is an elastic synthetic fiber created to add stretch to any fabric. Added to knit fabrics, the stretch can be as much as 100 percent, so it makes them perfect for form-fitted items like swimwear, activewear, and undergarments. Lycra can be stretched repeatedly and still recover its original length.

- **Weight.** Lycra is lightweight, soft, and smooth. However, it's also strong, durable, and tear and

Sophie looks playful, yet striking, in her gorgeous new winter accessories.

heat resistant. It can be made into finer yarns but also added, in small percentages, to thicker knits.

- **Fiber content.** Lycra is synthetic but can be added to any fabric blend including cotton, silk, and other synthetic fibers like polyester and nylon.

- **Stability.** The stability of the fabric depends on the other fiber content. Some swimwear materials curl slightly on the edges and others lay flat.

Lycra-blend fabrics are perfect for our *Swimsuit* (page 136) and *Leggings* (page 75). But don't be afraid to experiment: our *Not-So-Plain Tee* (page 102) made up in a Lycra blend would work as a wet-suit top for water sports, and our *Bubble Dress* (page 129) would look adorable for dancewear.

Tricot

- **Stretch.** Tricots generally have about 50-percent stretch across the grain.

- **Weight.** Tricot is lightweight and semi-sheer, which makes it appropriate for lingerie and lining specialty knits.

- **Fiber content.** Tricots are generally 100-percent nylon.

- **Stability.** They may curl slightly on the edges.

Tricot can be used as an optional lining for our *Swimsuit* pattern (page 136).

Stretch Velour and Stretch Velvet

- **Stretch.** Velour and stretch velvets generally stretch about 25 to 35 percent across the grain, or more if they contain a high level of Lycra.

- **Weight.** They're available in various weights. Stretch velour and stretch velvets have a soft brushed nap on the right side; velvet has a shinier appearance than velour. Due to the nap, all pattern pieces must be cut in the same direction.

- **Fiber content.** Stretch velour generally comes in either 100-percent polyester or an 80-percent cotton/20-percent poly blend. It may also contain a small amount of Lycra for added elasticity. Most stretch velvets I've found are either polyester or cotton with, anywhere from 3 to 10-percent Lycra.

- **Stability.** Depending on the fiber content, they may curl a bit on the cut edge. Sewing with these plush and slippery fabrics can be tricky. Make sure you place your pins closer together and hold your fabric tightly while sewing or serging. Check frequently as you sew to make sure the pieces have not shifted.

These super-soft and warm fabrics are perfect for the *Swim Cover-up* (page 144) and the *Contrast V-Neck Sweater* (page 108) but can also be used for the *Harlequin Quilt* (page 50), the *Stripwork Scarf* (page 37), and most of the tops and bottoms in this book.

Notion Devotion: Types of Stretch Trims and Notions

Ready for more stretching? No need to pull a muscle—I'm talking *stretch trims* and *notions*. When you're sewing with stretch fabrics, you have to keep in mind that any embellishments you add to your garment, if they run with the maximum stretch of the fabric, must also be stretchy. Nowadays, stretch notions go way beyond your plain old elastic, although plain old elastic is still quite necessary for anything from waistbands to headbands. Let's run through them from the most rudimentary to the most decorative.

Elastic

There are four basic categories of elastic: *woven, knitted, braided,* and *clear.* You can generally find them at the fabric stores in many different widths from a teeny-tiny $\frac{1}{16}$ inch to a hefty 2 inches, although manufacturers produce some of these elastics as wide as 18 inches—no joke!

- **Woven** elastic is the thickest of all four types and thus the strongest. It has both crosswise and lengthwise ribs, giving it a windowpane appearance. it is perfect to use for home décor projects and heavy-weight fabrics. Woven elastics do not narrow when stretched and can be used inside casings or stitched directly to the fabric.

- **Knitted** elastic is my favorite type to use for knit clothing. It's thinner and lighter than woven elastic, so it doesn't add extra bulk in waistbands, but is still very strong, so it'll easily hold up the weight of your sewn garment. Because it doesn't narrow when stretched, you can use it in casings or stitch directly on it.

- **Braided** elastic is a lightweight elastic that narrows when stretched, so you don't want to sew right on it because the needle would damage it. It's primarily used for swimwear and dancewear.

- **Clear** elastic isn't braided, knitted, or woven. It's a transparent, synthetic product that's used primarily to stabilize horizontal seams on garments sewn with lightweight stretch fabrics. If you have a purchased knit top, you can take a look inside and see if you spot any clear elastic or seam tape around the neck or shoulder seams. To apply clear elastic, you stitch it right into the seam as you're sewing the garment together.

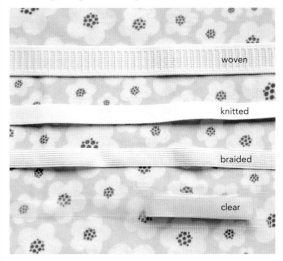

Elastic Sewing Thread

This is a wonderful product that is typically used for creating rows and rows of shirring (or stretchy gathers) on garments and accessories. You can find elastic thread at most fabric stores in the notions department, and it typically comes in a long spool like the one pictured. At my local fabric stores I've only seen elastic thread in black or white, but online I've found it in a variety of pretty colors. I usually buy two or three spools at a time because you'd be surprised at how fast you go through those 30 yards! The package comes with shirring instructions printed on the back, but for more detailed step-by-step instructions, see our Shirrley Tank Dress pattern (page 122).

Fold-Over Elastic

The day I discovered fold-over elastic, commonly referred to as FOE, I thought, "Where have you been all my life?" FOE is one of my favorite products to use for knitwear because of its versatility: It stretches like elastic so you can use it to create waistbands, but it's super soft and lightweight so you can also use it for infant headbands and it doesn't feel too tight or scratchy like other elastics do. And because it has such a smooth appearance, comes in a wide gamut of colors and prints, and has a noticeable groove down the middle, you can apply it to the fabric like binding, folding it over the edge of your fabric on anything from cloth diapers to swimwear (page 136).

I've never seen FOE sold at my local fabric stores, so I always turn to my favorite online sources for it (see "Resources" on page 155). If you can't find it at your usual independent quilt shops or online stores, try searching for it on Etsy or eBay. I guarantee you'll come up with hundreds of choices and since it weighs practically nothing, the shipping charges will be minimal.

Stretch Lace

Just like with elastic, stretch lace can be found in a variety of widths, colors, and textures. And just like with FOE, it may be difficult to find locally, but online sources will give you a wonderful variety of styles to choose from. I love using stretch lace to trim the hems on the Leggings (page 75) and Not-So-Plain Tee (page 102) but it is also great to use for shoulder straps, like on our Shirrley Tank Dress (page 122).

Other Stretch Trims

There are so many different types of decorative stretch trims that I couldn't possibly list them all, but some of my favorites are picot edge elastic, stretch ruffled organza, and ruffled elastic ribbon, all pictured below and all available in a variety of colors and styles. To apply these adorable trims to the hems of leggings, shorts, or tees, you can sew them right onto the raw edge of the fabric using a stretch or zigzag stitch on your sewing machine. Stretch the trim slightly as you stitch it down if you want the fabric to gather a bit at the edge.

CHAPTER 1

guide to sewing with knits

As my computer nerd husband says, "Software is the magic that makes the world go round. Hardware is the mechanism that allows the magic to become real." This logic can definitely be applied to sewing. Once you've chosen your project and purchased the correct fabrics and trims for it, if you're anything like me, you're itching to get started. However, there are a few more things you need to know before you begin. You'll soon find out that sewing with knits isn't scary or difficult after all and that just like with anything else, once you familiarize yourselves with the tools and processes, it becomes easy and fun. So, let's talk *hardware* for a bit, then we can let the magic unfold.

Tools of the Trade

We're not building a skyscraper here, so you don't need a crane or a bulldozer, but as you know, you need the right tools to do the job right. If you're an avid sewist, you'll be happy to know that, with the exception of one or two items, most of the tools I use for sewing with knits are probably already in your repertoire. However, if you're new to sewing, sit back, relax, and let me help you build the perfect sewing kit, no matter what type of fabrics you're using.

The Chopping Block

No sewing room should be without a good-quality rotary cutter, a plastic ruler, and a self-healing mat. These three amigos work in tandem for your cutting pleasure. Learn from my mistake and don't skimp on your rotary cutter. After a couple of years of poor cutting, I finally treated myself to an Olfa 45mm rotary cutter and I've never looked back. I also love the tiny blade of my 18mm cutter because it's perfect for cutting around tight curves like arm and neck openings. Always keep replacement blades on hand. As soon as your blade fails to cut cleanly through the fabric in one pass, replace it with a fresh one—your fingers will thank you!

To weigh down your pattern piece while you cut, you can buy special weights at the fabric store, but I use pretty much any small item I have at arm's reach . . . my magnetic pin holder is my favorite weight (I always keep a couple of those around) but I'll also admit to having used a pair of scissors, a tape dispenser, or even my cell phone in a pinch. I'm all about multipurpose items!

Even though I cut most of my garment pieces with my rotary cutter, I still use my scissors regularly, so it's a good idea to invest in a good pair of these since you'll notice right away how smoothly they cut and how sturdy they feel. I prefer 8-inch dressmaking shears with a bent handle for smooth cutting on flat surfaces, and a pair of 3½-inch or 4-inch embroidery scissors for smaller jobs. Embroidery scissors or thread nippers are great to keep next to your serger and sewing machine to snip off thread ends, but I also use them for notching outer curves, clipping inner curves, and trimming my corners before turning my pieces to avoid extra bulk in the seams.

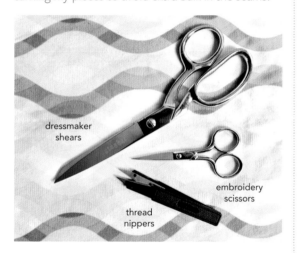

dressmaker shears

embroidery scissors

thread nippers

Keep a pair of paper-cutting scissors handy for cutting pattern sheets and *never,* ever, EVER use your dressmaking shears for cutting through paper—it will dull your blade, and you'll feel like a dullard in the process! My kids know all too well the wrath that will befall them if they ever lay a finger on my dressmaking shears. If your fabric and paper scissors can be easily mistaken for one another, it's customary to tie a small piece of ribbon on the fabric shears' handle to differentiate them from others.

Needling You

I always keep a large supply of sewing machine needles around because invariably your needle will break in the middle of a project (happens to all of us) and the last thing you want to do is run to the store to fetch a new one. Always use a ballpoint needle to sew on knits. It has a rounded tip that allows the needle to pass through knit fabric without cutting the yarns. The universal needles you normally use for most sewing projects will cut or catch the yarns and leave tiny holes in your garment that will eventually turn into big, unsightly runs.

For delicate knits, use needle size 70/10. For medium thickness knits, like most interlocks and jerseys, use needle size 80/12. For thick knits, like stretch velour, stretch velvets, and double knits, use needle size 90/14. Typically, the thicker the fabric, the higher the needle number (shank thickness) you'll need. For very stretchy fabrics, like swimsuit Lycra, use a stretch needle. If you're using a twin needle for hemming your knit garments, make sure you purchase a stretch twin (see the section, "The Grand Finale," on page 26).

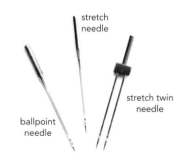

stretch needle

stretch twin needle

ballpoint needle

If you're sewing with a serger, you don't need to run out and buy all new needles for your knits. Sergers come already equipped with a "semi-ballpoint" needle, which can be used successfully for all types of fabrics. If those needles break on you, replace them with the same types of needles, usually available through your serger dealer.

Of course, if you've taken all the care in the world to use the right kind of needle for your knit projects, it would be silly to use the wrong straight pins. Get yourself a box of ballpoint pins and mark them well so you don't confuse them later with the regular pins. I keep two different colors of magnetic pin holders on my sewing table at all times—this way I always know that my lavender holder has the ballpoint pins and my red one holds the regular pins.

The Common Thread

You should use all-purpose polyester threads for sewing with knits as they are stronger and have a bit more stretch than the 100-percent cotton ones. I always keep a few spools of the colors I use the most on hand so I don't risk running out in the middle of a project. If you're sewing strictly with a sewing machine, I recommend picking up a spool of textured thread, like Woolly Nylon, Polyarn, or

Bulky Nylon. Use it in the bobbin to give your seams maximum elasticity.

If you're sewing with a serger, you will need to invest in serger spools and textured thread for your rolled hems. (More on that in the "Sewing Knits with Your Serger" section on page 25.)

Measuring Up

Keep a flexible tape measure handy for measuring your child, yourself, or the garment pieces as you're sewing. Also, throw a retractable tape measure in your purse; it always comes in handy when you're at the fabric store!

The Turning Point

You need a good turning tool to help you turn straps, belts, loops, or any small, skinny piece that can't be easily turned right side out with your fingers. There are tons of tools available for this purpose, but my favorite isn't one that I bought at a fabric store. I use surgical forceps or a clamp, also called a *hemostat*, because it's narrow enough to fit through even the tightest of spaces, it clamps on to the fabric tightly, and has a scissor-like handle that helps you pull the piece right side out effortlessly. But best of all, it doesn't pierce the fabric at all in the process, which is something that can't be said about most turning tools sold at fabric stores.

I bought my first hemostat on Amazon.com for just under eight dollars then a couple of months later I saw them at a local craft fair on a tool table for only two dollars, so I got a couple more of different sizes. So, run out and buy one right now—you will thank me later! By the way, I can't take credit for this genius idea. I first read about this on one of my favorite crafty Web sites, Sew4Home.com.

To get your corners nice and pointy on garment pieces, pillows, quilts, and so on, you need a blunt tool like a bone creaser, but I prefer to use a pair of wooden chopsticks for this purpose. The narrow point on a chopstick is small enough to push the fabric out on the corners of your piece but not so narrow that it'll break through the seam. I told you I like multipurpose tools!

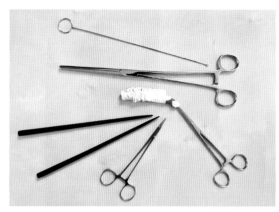

In addition to the tools detailed in the previous sections, no sewing kit is complete without the following essentials:

- **Seam ripper**—a necessary evil!
- **Safety pins of various sizes**—you'll use these to help insert elastic through casings.
- **Water-soluble fabric marker or chalk pencil**—to transfer pattern markings (notches, button, or pocket positioning, and so on) to the fabric.
- **Seam and hem gauges**—to help you get that perfectly even hem.
- **Extra bobbins**—keep them loaded with all of your favorite thread colors and load one with elastic thread.

So, now that your sewing kit is fully stocked, let's learn the basics of sewing knits with your sewing machine and serger.

Sewing Knits with Your Sewing Machine

One of the biggest misconceptions about sewing with knits is that you'll need a serger. This idea keeps many sewists from experimenting with knits, because they fear the expense of new equipment. The good news is that you don't need a serger to sew with knits, so get your sewing machine out and let's review a few basic rules.

The key to sewing with stretch fabrics is that your stitches must also be stretchy so that you can actually pull the garment over your head and shoulders without popping a seam. Of course, overlock machines (sergers) are ideal for this because they automatically create a seam that's stretchy (see the "Sewing Knits with Your Serger," section on the next page for more info), but you can do the same with your sewing machine. And no, you do *not* need a brand new, fancy-schmancy, computerized machine. If your machine can do a zigzag stitch—and, even the most basic machines can—you can sew with knits!

A zigzag stitch has some give, which is really all you need to have a functioning stretch seam. Newer machines come equipped with a *two-step* and *three-step zigzag* that are specifically designed for stretch fabrics, and some even come with a *stem* or *stretch* stitch (the one that looks like a lightning bolt) which, again, is ideal for knits. If you're using a regular zigzag stitch, to reduce bulk in your seams, use a very narrow width (no more than 1mm) and a slightly longer stitch length (about 3mm). Consult your sewing machine manual to see what kinds of stretch stitches it comes with, and if you are still unsure, don't be afraid to ask for assistance at your local independent fabric store. In my experience, I've found that the women who work at these stores are highly knowledgeable and always willing and able to give advice.

Once you've determined which stitch you're using for your garment construction (zigzag, three-step-zigzag, or stem), the next step is to make sure you have the right needles and thread. Refer to the "Needling You" section on page 21 for a more in-depth description of these supplies, but just to summarize, you'll need ballpoint needles and polyester threads. You can also use textured threads in the bobbin for added elasticity, but it's certainly not necessary.

Now that you've selected your stitch and have your machine loaded with the proper needles and thread, it's time to get sewing. Feed your fabric nice and steady. Do *not* stretch it at all while sewing or you'll end up with a wavy seam. If you were sewing knits with a straight stitch, you would definitely need to stretch the fabric as you sew to keep the seams from popping later, but I don't recommend that method. If you have trouble keeping your fabric from stretching while sewing, adjust the tension on your machine or switch to a walking foot (like the kind quilters use). It's a good idea to practice on some scrap fabric before sewing the garment to make sure all your settings are correct. Always backstitch at the beginning and end of every seam to reinforce your stitch and make sure the threads don't come unraveled. Finally, press well after every step to make sure your garment maintains its shape and doesn't get distorted.

To Press or To Iron, What is the Difference?

When you iron, you glide the iron back and forth along the garment, but this can easily stretch and distort the fabric, especially if it's knit. To press, you lift and place your iron over the fabric, preferably on the wrong side, applying gentle pressure to seams and hems, but never gliding it across the surface. I recommend always pressing, not ironing, your knit fabric during garment construction.

Sewing Knits with Your Serger

If you're an occasional sewist who only sews once in a while—purely for fun—you can certainly get by with a conventional sewing machine. However, if you intend to sew knits on a regular basis or sew for profit, I strongly recommend that you invest on a good quality serger (also called an overlocker if you're in the

U.K.). An inexpensive serger can cost around $200 to $400; it will seem fine at first, but you'll be pulling your hair out every time you have to deal with skipped stitches, chewed up fabric edges, or thread jams. Oh, and believe me, some of those serger jams are bad enough to put even Mother Teresa in the nuthouse! A good quality serger can run anywhere from $800 to $1,500, but trust me when I say it is money well spent and you'll only have to spend it once. And if you decide to splurge on a Baby Lock serger like I did, you'll agree that the jet-air threading itself is worth every penny you spent. But don't get discouraged if your serger doesn't have jet-air threading; all sergers come with a color-coded threading chart, usually located on the inside of the door. That guide will help you figure out what goes where.

The main benefit of a serger is that it sews your seams, trims the excess fabric, and *overlocks* (finishes) the edge all in one pass so it saves you tons of time. You do not have to sew and then serge—Genius! All the garments in this book can be made entirely with a serger, with the exception of a few techniques, like shirring, topstitching, and hemming. You can even attach elastic and stretch trims to your garment with your serger. And, best of all, some of the newer, more expensive sergers come with a coverstitch function so that you can even hem your garments with it. How cool is that?

It's important to keep your serger manual handy at all times because, until you become familiar with it, you'll need to reference the manual for anything from threading it to switching functions (like from overlock to rolled hem and back). And like all machinery, whether it's your car, your computer, or your serger, you will eventually experience technical difficulties, so it's important to familiarize yourself with all its parts and how they work—but when all else fails, call tech support.

Sergers use serger cones, which are much bigger than the regular thread spools that you're used to, but also more expensive. The thread is essentially the same, so if you don't want to splurge on a bunch of different colors of serger cones (since you need to buy four at a time!), you can get by with using regular thread spools for the needle threads and serger cones for the upper and lower loopers. You can use regular spools for all of them, actually, but you'll notice that the loopers use up so much thread that your spool will be empty in no time. Just make sure you place spool caps over your standard spools (those should come with the serger) to help hold the spool on the thread stand and help feed the thread evenly through the path.

Occasionally, I like to use a textured thread on my upper looper, especially when doing rolled hems or lettuce edges. You can read more about these in the following section.

As you already read in the section, "Tools of the Trade," the needles that came with your serger are "semi-ballpoint" needles, so you don't need to run out and buy new ones for serging on knits. When those needles are dull or break, replace them with the same types of needles, which are usually found through your serger dealer.

TIP: As a rule of thumb, change your machine's needles every third sewing project, or 12 hours of usage, whichever comes first, to avoid skipped stitches.

The Grand Finale: Finishing Techniques

All great performances end with a spectacular closing scene. And if you're like me, your newest creation always seems like your best performance yet (until the next one, of course). So let's finish off this show with a bang . . . *or a hem!* Here are the nominees for *Best Hemming Techniques for Knit Garments*, from the most professional to the easiest.

Coverstitch

This is the twin or triple needle stitching that you see on the hems of most ready-to-wear (RTW) knit garments. The top (right side) looks like parallel rows of straight stitching, and the underside looks like serger loops that cover the folded raw edge. A coverstitch machine is needed for this. However, many top-of-the-line sergers have a coverstitch function.

To finish your garment using this technique, fold the hem toward the wrong side and press well. I like to use a ½-inch hem, but you can use any width hem according to your preference. Feed the garment onto the coverstitch machine right side up (in other words, with the folded raw edge on the underside) and align your left needle with the half-inch mark. Don't stretch the fabric at all while you feed it. If sewing in the round, overlap your stitches slightly and leave some long tails at the end. Using a hand-sewing needle, bring the top threads to the underside and tie a couple of knots to secure your stitching.

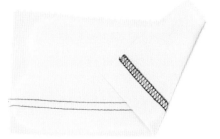

Rolled Hem

 A rolled hem is a narrow, dense stitch made on the edge of the fabric. If you own a serger, a rolled hem is a quick and easy way to finish a knit garment and a great way to add pizzazz by using a contrasting thread color. Make sure you use a textured thread, like Woolly Nylon, Polyarn, or Bulky Nylon, on the upper looper to get that thick, rich-looking rolled hem.

To finish your garment with this technique, follow your serger's instructions for a three-thread rolled hem. Each serger model is different, but all models will require that you remove your left needle so you'll

only be sewing with the right one. Your manual will tell you how to set your stitch length and width in order to get a perfect rolled hem, but you should always practice on a scrap of fabric, moving the dials back and forth until you get it exactly as you like it. The objective is to have little to no spacing in between the stitches. Your serger will fold under the fabric and create a $\frac{1}{16}$ inch-overedge hem.

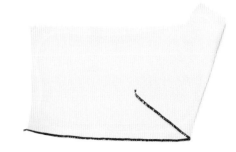

Lettuce Edge

While doing a rolled hem, if you set your serger's differential feed to maximum stretch and also stretch the fabric slightly with your fingers while you feed it through, it'll give the edge of your garment a wavy, ruffled finish like lettuce leaves.

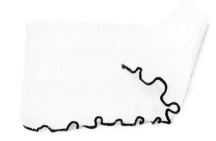

Faux-Coverstitch

Fool even the most discerning eye into thinking you finished your garment with a coverstitch machine by using a stretch twin needle on your sewing machine.

To achieve this look, press your hem up toward the wrong side ½ inch. Loosen up your machine's tension a bit, to avoid getting a tunneling effect. With a medium-to-long stitch length and using your twin needle, stitch your hem down from the right side of the garment. Make sure you use a textured thread, like Woolly Nylon, Polyarn, or Bulky Nylon, in the bobbin to give your hems maximum elasticity. From the right side of the garment, your hem will look just like a coverstitched hem with two rows of perfectly spaced straight stitches, but on the underside, you'll see a zigzag stitch where your bobbin thread crosses back and forth.

Zigzag Stitch

For a funky, homemade look, press your hem up towards the wrong side ½ inch. Set your sewing machine to a zigzag stitch at a medium stitch length and stitch your hem down from the right side of the garment. Use a textured thread, like Woolly Nylon, Polyarn, or Bulky Nylon, in the bobbin to give your hems maximum elasticity, and always use a ballpoint needle when sewing with knits.

Raw Edge

For a more shabby-chic or grungy look, leave your hems unfinished on your knit garments. Your knit fabrics will not ravel but the raw edges might curl up a bit over time, depending on the type of knit fabric you used.

TIP: If you're interested in seeing these techniques in action, go to my Web site at modkidboutique.com and click the YouTube icon at the bottom. This will take you straight to my video channel where you can view a series of instructional videos I've created on hemming techniques.

Sign Your Work

Since every garment you create is a little masterpiece, why not put your signature on it? And if you're sewing for profit, this is even more important. It helps strengthen your brand while helping customers identify your work later on and come back for more. Garment tags come in all shapes, sizes, and styles to fit every budget. Look on etsy.com to find a myriad of clothing tag vendors that will create one to suit your style. You can upload your logo, pick a font from their library, or even have them design a logo for you if you don't have your brand identity quite figured out yet. If you're looking for a more polished and professional look, opt for a woven tag made from damask, taffeta, or satin. These won't fade or ravel in the wash so they're as permanent as the item they're sewn on. Search online for "woven clothing labels," but be sure to ask for samples and get quotes up front. My MODKID clothing labels and side seam inserts are made by a company out of Thailand called Lucky Label (www.luckylabel.com). I'm very happy with their service and quality.

CHAPTER 2

accessories

· · · ·

Sydney's Rosy Headband is made with my Lime Blossoms cotton interlock accented with rolled roses in a gorgeous, textured sweater knit that I had in my stash.

rosy headband

NOTES ON FIT: Our Rosy Headband comes in two sizes. The Small has a finished length of 31″ and is 3″ wide at its widest point. This would be perfect for toddlers and little girls up to 4 years old. The Large headband, for girls ages 5 and up, has a finished length of 33″ and is 4″ wide at its widest point.

Headbands are a Hollywood craze that keeps popping back up year after year—always a new style on the horizon. But it's not surprising. After all, isn't accessorizing the best part of dressing up? Give your little star in the making her own set of *Rosy Headbands* that she can mix and match with her new Modkid wardrobe. A jersey headband will be perfect for school, play dates, and casual parties. For those dressy affairs, make her a Rosy Headband out of stretch velvet or organic velour to really glam it up. And if you're new to sewing with knits, this is the perfect starter project— easy, simple, and quick!

SUPPLIES

You can use most stretch fabrics for your Rosy Headband including, but not limited to, cotton interlock, jerseys, double knits, rib knits, stretch velvet, or stretch velour. For our sample headbands, we used a 100-percent cotton interlock for the main headband piece and a glittery sweater knit for the rolled roses. Refer to page 10 for more information on types of knits.

Use Pattern Piece A on page 1.

- ¼ yard of knit fabric for size Small headband OR ⅓ yard for size Large headband
- Scraps of decorative/textured knit at least 10″ wide for rolled roses
- Matching thread
- Sewing needle for hand work
- Rotary cutter, straightedge ruler, and self-healing mat; or dressmaking shears

CUT

1 Fold the knit fabric in half so the selvedges meet on one side, and cut 2 of Pattern Piece A on the fold as shown in figure 1.

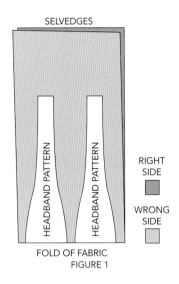

SELVEDGES

RIGHT SIDE

WRONG SIDE

HEADBAND PATTERN

HEADBAND PATTERN

FOLD OF FABRIC
FIGURE 1

2 Cut out 3, 2½″ × 10″ strips of textured knit fabric for rolled roses on the lengthwise grain (figure 2). You can also cut strips out on the widthwise grain, depending on your fabric selection—look at your fabric pattern/design to determine placement.

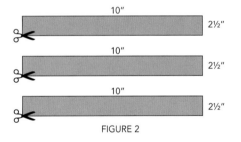

10″   2½″

10″   2½″

10″   2½″

FIGURE 2

ASSEMBLE

3 Pin the headband pieces right sides together. Using a stretch or zigzag stitch on your sewing machine and a ½″ seam allowance, stitch the headband along the perimeter, leaving a 2″ gap on one side for turning (figure 3).

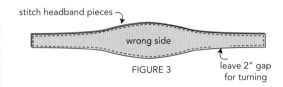

stitch headband pieces

wrong side

FIGURE 3   leave 2″ gap for turning

4 Turn the headband right side out, press flat, and slipstitch the opening closed with your hand needle and thread (figure 4). Place the headband aside while you create the rolled roses.

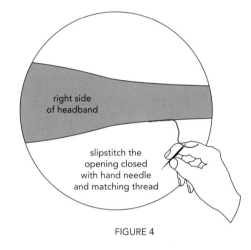

right side of headband

slipstitch the opening closed with hand needle and matching thread

FIGURE 4

5 Fold the 2½″ × 10″ strips in half lengthwise and press. Trim the short ends of the fabric to a gentle curve as shown in figure 5.

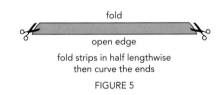

fold

open edge

fold strips in half lengthwise then curve the ends

FIGURE 5

6 Using matching thread and a hand needle, thread your needle with double thread and knot the end. Create long basting stitches to gather the fabric along the 10″ length, stitching along the open side, not the folded side, of the strip (figure 6).

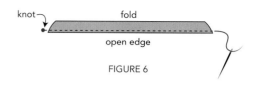

knot fold open edge

FIGURE 6

7 Once you have stitched the strip, leave the needle connected to the strip. Start gathering the fabric by gently pulling the thread with your fingers while you hold the fabric strip on the other hand—the fold of the fabric should be on the top of the flower. Roll the gathered edge around onto itself until the shape of the rose starts to form, and finish by hand-stitching through the bottom side of the "roll" several times to secure the fabric.

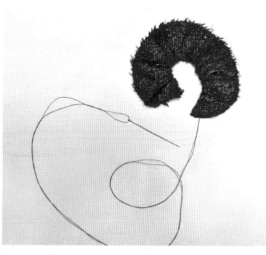

Gently pull on the threads with your hand to begin gathering the fabric.

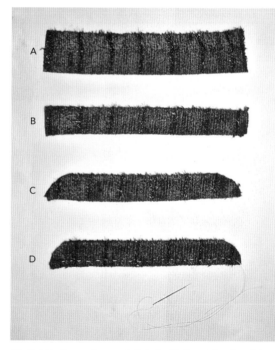

A) Cut 1 piece of stretch fabric 2½" × 10". B) Fold the strip in half lengthwise. C) Round the short edges. D) Sew a running stitch across the open sides with a hand needle and double thread.

With the gathered edge at the bottom and folded edge at the top, begin rolling the fabric around itself to create the rose shape.

TIP: Feel free to stitch a cute button, pearl, or bead to the center of the rolled roses for that extra touch of whimsy.

Pinch the bottom of the rolled rose with one hand while tightly rolling the fabric with the other.

After you have rolled the entire strip into a rose shape, hand-stitch a few times across the bottom edges to secure the strip in place and keep it from unrolling.

8   Pin the rolled roses in the desired position on the headband. Use a hand needle with double thread to tack the flowers to the headband (figure 7).

FIGURE 7

Sophie's Rosy Headband and Mondrian Shirt (page 97) are made with a combination of cotton interlocks in tones of black, gray, and hot pink for a touch of sophistication.

stripwork scarf

6" wide × 62" long

NOTES ON FIT: The final length of this scarf is 62" long if you are cutting the strips the full width of a 58"-wide knit fabric. If you desire a shorter scarf, you can easily shorten the length by cutting the strips shorter.

Keep your little snow bunny warm and cozy during those cold, wintry days with our stylish *Stripwork Scarf*. If your kids are anything like mine, they always forget to grab their scarves before heading out, so I had to dream up a way for them to actually *want* to show off their winter gear. I let the girls pick out their favorite fabrics and designed a scarf for them that's festive, playful, and fun—it's *their* little creation! We made ours using interlock cottons because they are so soft, fairly light, and come in a plethora of fun designs, but if you're looking for an extra layer of good-looking warmth, try making your scarf out of organic velour, stretch velvet, or fleece.

SUPPLIES

You can use most stretch fabrics for your Stripwork Scarf including, but not limited to, cotton interlock, jerseys, double knits, rib knits, stretch velvet, or stretch velour, 58"/60" wide. Refer to page 10 for more information on types of knits.

There are no pattern pieces for this project.

- ½ yard of two different knit fabrics (or use remnants of several different fabric prints for a funkier look)
- Coordinating thread
- Rotary cutter, straightedge ruler, and self-healing mat; or dressmaking shears

CUT

To achieve the look of our sample scarves, cut 4 pieces of fabric #1 selvedge to selvedge and 2½" wide. Cut 4 pieces of fabric #2 selvedge to selvedge and 2½" wide. You should have eight strips total, four of each fabric design. For your ruffle ends, cut 2 pieces 8" high × 22" wide (figure 1). Don't be afraid to mix it up and use alternating colors from your strips or a completely different coordinating fabric.

Sydney is stylish, comfy, and warm in her new Modkid winter ensemble consisting of a Stripwork Scarf, Rosy Headband (page 32), and A-Line Gored Skirt (page 80).

Cut 4 strips of fabric #1
2½" X 58"

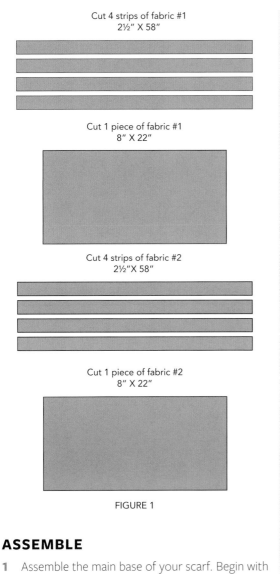

Cut 1 piece of fabric #1
8" X 22"

Cut 4 strips of fabric #2
2½"X 58"

Cut 1 piece of fabric #2
8" X 22"

FIGURE 1

ASSEMBLE

1   Assemble the main base of your scarf. Begin with a strip of fabric #1 and fabric #2. Stitch/serge right sides together along the length of the strips (figure 2). Press the seam to one side if serged, or press it open if stitched.

stitch/serge 1st strip to 2nd strip along the long edges
FIGURE 2

2   Stitch/serge the remainder of the strips, alternating between fabric #1 and fabric #2 until you have all eight strips stitched together in a row (figure 3).

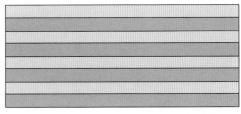

stitch/serge remaining strips alternating colors/fabrics
FIGURE 3

3   Fold the stripwork panel in half lengthwise, right sides together, to form a long tube, and close up the sides by stitching the first strip to the last along the side edge (figure 4). Turn the scarf right side out, and press.

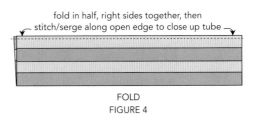

fold in half, right sides together, then stitch/serge along open edge to close up tube
FOLD
FIGURE 4

4   Now, let's create the ruffles by folding each ruffle piece right sides together, and stitching/serging along the 8″ side edges to create a circular band (figure 5).

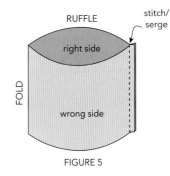

RUFFLE
stitch/serge
right side
FOLD
wrong side
FIGURE 5

5 Fold the circular band down in half lengthwise, wrong sides together, encasing the seam, as shown in figure 6, and press the fold at the top to create a nice crease. Your band should now be 4″ high × 21″ wide all around (or 4″ high × 10½″ wide folded).

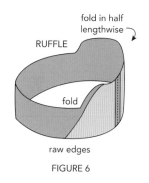

FIGURE 6

6 Run two lines of gathering stitches close to the raw edge of the ruffle band and pull to gather to the same width as the main scarf panel (roughly 6″ wide or 12″ all around) (figure 7).

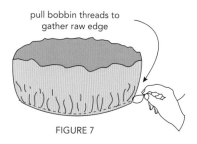

FIGURE 7

7 Attach the ruffles to the stripwork scarf. Lay your ruffle pieces over the right side of each scarf edge, aligning the seams and keeping the raw edges even. Pin in place all around and stitch or serge ½″ from the raw edges (figure 8). Fold the ruffles out and press the seams toward the inside of the scarf tube. If desired, topstitch the seam down using a coverstitch or zigzag stitch on your sewing machine.

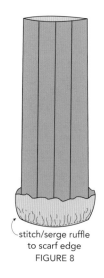

stitch/serge ruffle
to scarf edge
FIGURE 8

Picture perfect! Sophie strikes a pose in her new Stripwork Scarf and Rosy Headband (page 32) made with cotton interlocks.

fingerless gloves

NOTES ON FIT: You and your child are the designers on this project. The length and width of the glove are completely up to you, as are the fabric combinations. Have fun with it and let your kids express their creative side!

When the forecast calls for severe thunderstorms, I always find myself scrambling for a creative activity to keep the kids occupied at home. One of my favorite projects, my *Fingerless Gloves,* takes no more than an hour to complete and it's a great way to involve the kids on rainy days or birthdays. But the best part is that it's not gender or age specific—boys and girls, toddlers, and teenagers alike can have fun with this easy craft and you'll finally use up those fabric scraps piling up in your craft room. And, whether your kid is the "peace out" type or the "talk to the hand" type, this is the perfect all-seasons fashion accessory.

SUPPLIES

You can use any stretch fabrics for this project including, but not limited to, cotton interlock, jersey, double knits, stretch velour, stretch velvet, stretch fleece, or even dancewear/activewear fabrics. The more Lycra the fabric has, the tighter the fit. We used cotton interlock for our gloves and rib knits for the cuffs. Refer to page 10 for more information on types of knits.

There are no pattern pieces for this project. You will just trace your child's hand to make a paper template.

- Knit fabric scraps at least 12″ long × 6″ wide each
- Paper and pencil for tracing your child's hand
- Paper scissors for cutting out your paper template
- Coordinating thread
- Rotary cutter and self-healing mat, or dressmaking shears

MAKE THE PAPER TEMPLATE

1 Trace your child's hand onto a piece of paper. Make sure the fingers are spread open as wide as possible and trace all the way up to the middle of his/her arm (you can always trim the gloves down to size later).

Tween fashionista, Maddie, plays a game of "paparazzi" in her funky fingerless gloves.

2 Using a ruler or seam gauge, measure ½″ out from the traced hand line and draw a "cutting line" to create the seam allowance. When you get to the thumb, draw a straight line across the knuckle to mark where you will be "cutting it off" and then continue drawing the seam allowance around the fingers. It will be difficult to add a full ½″ seam allowance between the fingers, so you can just draw a line straight across the knuckles, and then draw a vertical line to divide each finger as shown in figure 1. This should give you at least ¼″ of ease in between the fingers.

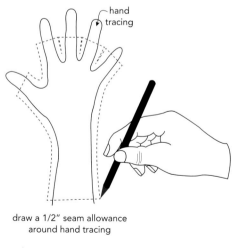

draw a 1/2″ seam allowance
around hand tracing

FIGURE 1

3 Cut your paper template on the new line (with seam allowances added). This will be your Fingerless Gloves pattern (figure 2).

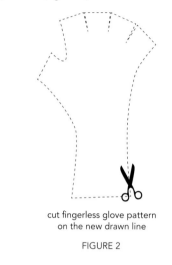

cut fingerless glove pattern
on the new drawn line

FIGURE 2

CUT

4 Fold the fabric right sides together so the selvedges meet on one side, and then cut your glove pattern out, creating the two sides to the glove. The maximum stretch of the fabric should go widthwise across the glove (figure 3). You will need two glove pieces for each fingerless glove you want to make.

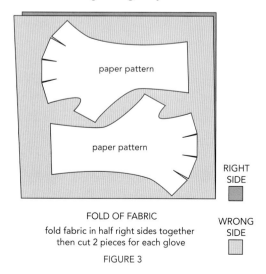

FOLD OF FABRIC
fold fabric in half right sides together
then cut 2 pieces for each glove

FIGURE 3

RIGHT
SIDE

WRONG
SIDE

ASSEMBLE

5 With the glove pieces right sides together, pin and begin stitching them only ¼" from the edge using a tiny zigzag stitch or a stretch stitch on your sewing machine. Leave the thumb and finger openings unstitched. When you get to the areas between the fingers, stitch as close to the dividing line as possible (figure 4). Always remember to backstitch a couple of times at the end of your stitches to reinforce those areas. This is especially important around the thumb and finger openings, since you are not hemming them.

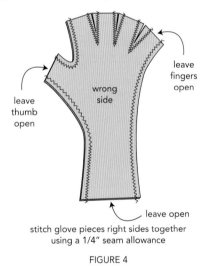

stitch glove pieces right sides together
using a 1/4" seam allowance

FIGURE 4

6 Turn the glove right side out and have your child try it on for fit. If the fingers are too long, mark the desired length with a fabric marker and then trim to size. Also, if the glove feels too loose, you can run a second line of stitching just barely inside the first one to tighten it up. Reinforce those finger openings again with a few overlapping stitches.

7 Now, let's make a small cuff for your glove using rib knit or a thick interlock. I like using a solid or contrasting fabric. Measure the width of your glove all around the arm opening and add ½" for the seam allowances. This is the length of your cuff. The width of the cuff should be 2½". Cut 1 cuff for each glove, making sure to keep the maximum stretch of the fabric going widthwise (figure 5).

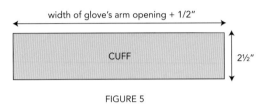

FIGURE 5

8 Fold the cuff piece onto itself right sides together and stitch/serge along the short side with a ¼" seam allowance, creating a circular band. If you used a sewing machine, press the seams open, and if you used a serger, press the seam to one side (figure 6).

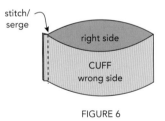

FIGURE 6

9 Fold the cuff down in half, wrong sides together, and press, creating a finished folded edge and two raw edges, as shown in figure 7.

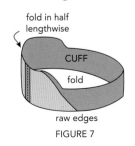

FIGURE 7

10 With your glove right side out, place the cuff over the arm opening, aligning the cuff seam with the inner seam of the glove and keeping the raw edges even. Pin in place all around, stretching the raw edges of the cuff slightly to fit if necessary. Zigzag stitch or serge ¼″ from the raw edges (figure 8). Press the cuff outward and the seam allowance inward and you're done!

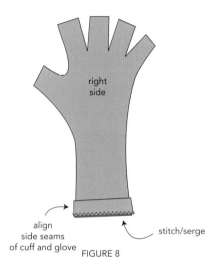

right side

align
side seams
of cuff and glove FIGURE 8

stitch/serge

Sophie's gloves are made with stretch denim and a contrasting rib knit.

Emersyn, Maddie, and Sophie pair their Leg Warmers up with our Not-So-Plain Tee (page 102) and Fingerless Gloves (page 41) for a complete funked-out ensemble.

leg warmers

NOTES ON FIT: Our Leg Warmers pattern was designed in three basic sizes: Small (2T–4T), Medium (5T–7), and Large (8–10). However, it's very easy to modify this pattern based on the size of your girl by just adding or subtracting length to the middle panel. Likewise, if you want the cuffs to be a little tighter or looser, you can easily add or subtract fabric to the width of these panels. Every child is unique, so don't be afraid to modify this pattern to fit your child.

The 80s. It was a fun time to be growing up. I fondly remember the emergence of MTV and great movies like *Flashdance* and *Fame*. Those movies weren't just fun—they triggered the leg warmer fashion craze, which I was happy to be a part of. Now I'm thrilled to see they're making a comeback. So thrilled, in fact, that I present you with my version of the knit *Leg Warmers*. They sew up in a snap and go perfectly with some designer jeans or paired up with our Leggings pattern. So, get that special girl of yours in a retro mood with some cool leg warmers and let's play some Pac-Man!

				Cutting Guide for Leg Warmers		
	US Size	EURO Size	FINISHED LENGTH	TOP CUFF CUT 2 PIECES	CENTER PANEL CUT 2 PIECES	BOTTOM CUFF CUT 2 PIECES
S	2T - 4T	92 -104	8"	4.5"h x 8.5"w	6"h x 10"w	3"h x 6"w
M	5T - 7	110 -122	10"	5"h x 9.5"w	8"h x 11"w	3"h x 7"w
L	8 - 10	128 -140	12"	6"h x 10.5"w	10"h x 12"w	3"h x 8"w

Child Sizing Chart

SUPPLIES

You can use most stretch fabrics for your Leg Warmers including, but not limited to, cotton interlock, jersey, rib knits, stretch velvet, or stretch velour, 58"/60" wide. I recommend that you use a thicker, stretchier fabric (like a rib knit) for the cuffs because they will hug the leg better instead of slouching down. Refer to page 10 for more information on types of knits.

No pattern pieces are necessary. Use the cutting guide provided above.

- ¼ yard of knit fabric for the center panel (all sizes)
- ⅛ yard of ribbing (rib knits) for the cuffs (all sizes)
- Coordinating thread
- Rotary cutter and self-healing mat, or dressmaking shears
- **OPTIONAL:** stretch trims (stretch lace, stretch ribbon, knit ruffles, and so on) to embellish leg warmers

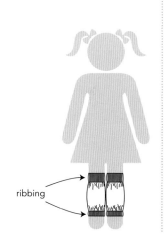

ribbing

CUT

Refer to the cutting guide provided on the previous page to determine what size to cut each leg warmer piece. Remember that the maximum stretch of the fabric should always go side-to-side on all of these panels. You should have two center panels, two top cuffs, and two bottom cuffs.

ASSEMBLE

1   Begin by sewing each piece into a tube. Fold each piece onto itself, right sides together, making sure to keep the maximum stretch of the fabric going side-to-side, and stitch/serge along the side raw edges, creating a circular band. If you used a sewing machine, go ahead and press the seams open, and if you used a serger, press the seams to one side (figure 1).

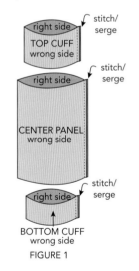

FIGURE 1

2   Turn the center panel right side out and lay it aside for now. Then fold each cuff down in half, wrong sides together, and press, creating a finished folded edge and two raw edges, as shown in figure 2. The seam you created in step 1 will now be encased within the cuff.

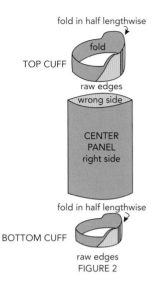

FIGURE 2

3   With your center panel right side out, place one cuff over the center panel, aligning the seams and keeping the raw edges even. Pin in place all around, stretching the raw edges of the cuff slightly to fit.

TIP: It helps to divide each piece into quarters, pin them together at those spots and stretch them in between to get an even stretch throughout.

4   Stitch or serge ½" from the raw edges (figure 3). Repeat for the bottom cuff. Press well and you're done!

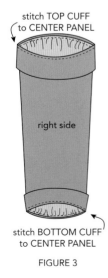

FIGURE 3

We love the look of these sweet leg warmers made with organic stretch velour (so soft!) and coordinating rib knits for the cuffs.

The girls love how soft this quilt turned out, and especially that it's big enough for all of them to play on.

harlequin quilt

FINISHED SIZE

48″ × 65″

Quilts can't be made with knits? Pshaw! We make quilts to keep us warm and snuggly, and what better material to do that with than layer upon layer of soft cotton interlock. I'll never forget the first time I saw a knit quilt (yes, I admit I didn't invent this). It was at the Spring 2010 International Quilt Market where I was debuting my first line of 100-percent cotton interlocks with Michael Miller Fabrics. Ellen Maxwell, a wonderful lady and expert quilter, brought a quilt she had designed with my knits for me to use in a presentation I was giving. Well, my voice could barely be heard over the *oohs* and *ahs* from the audience as the quilt was passed around to feel the softness. I knew right then and there that a simple quilt project with knits was a must for this book. And so you have it, the *Harlequin Quilt*!

SUPPLIES

You can use most stretch fabrics for your Harlequin Quilt including, but not limited to, cotton interlock, matte jerseys, double knits, stretch velvet, or stretch velour. Look for good quality knits with 25 to 50-percent stretch, great recovery, and no curl on the edges.

Use Template Pieces A (flower petals) and B (flower center) on page 3.

- 1 yard of 58″/60″-wide knit fabric of color A
- 1 yard of 58″/60″-wide knit fabric of color B
- ¼ yard of knit fabric each, of colors C and D for flower appliqués
- 2 yards of 56″/58″-wide knit fabric for quilt backing (can be of color A, B, C, or D as desired)
- Coordinating thread
- Straightedge ruler, rotary cutter, and self-healing mat for cutting straight pieces
- Lightweight fusible web or quilt basting spray for fusing flower appliqués to quilt
- A dinner plate and fabric-soluble marker for marking rounded corners
- Masking tape and pen for labeling pieces

- **OPTIONAL:** 2 yards cotton quilt batting or fleece. You can make this quilt with or without the batting, but if you decide to use batting, the fusible kind, like Fusi-Boo by Fairfield, is ideal for this project.

CUT

Refer to figure 1:

- Cut 12 squares, 12″ × 12″, of fabric color A

- Cut 12 squares, 12″ × 12″, of fabric color B

- Cut 4 flower petals out of color C using **template A,** and 4 flower centers out of color D using **template B.** The best way to cut these appliqués is to trace the templates provided onto the paper side of a sheet of lightweight fusible web, then iron the sticky side of the fusible web to the back side of the fabric and cut the flowers and centers right on the traced line. This way, your appliqués will be ready to fuse to the quilt top after the quilt is finished.

- Cut 1 piece the full width of the fabric, approximately 58″ wide × 70″ high for quilt backing.

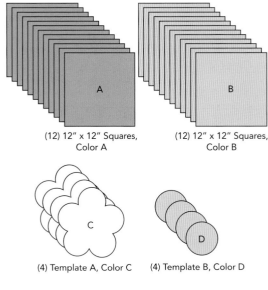

(12) 12″ x 12″ Squares, Color A

(12) 12″ x 12″ Squares, Color B

(4) Template A, Color C   (4) Template B, Color D

FIGURE 1

SUB-CUT

1   Take 1 square piece of color A and mark an X shape from corner to corner with a fabric-soluble marker. Using your straightedge ruler and a rotary cutter, cut along the lines that divide your square into four small triangles, as shown in figure 2. These will be the four corner pieces of your quilt.

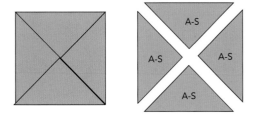

FIGURE 2

2   Take 5 squares of color A and mark a diagonal straight line from one corner to the other only. Using your straightedge ruler and a rotary cutter, cut along the line that divides your square into two large triangles, as shown in figure 3. These will be your top, bottom, and side pieces. You should have 10 equal-sized triangles.

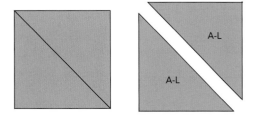

FIGURE 3

You should now have:

- 12 full squares of color B

- 6 full squares of color A

- 10 large triangles of color A (we'll call these "A-L" for A-Large)

- 4 small triangles of color A (we'll call these "A-S" for A-Small)

ASSEMBLE

3   Begin assembling your quilt top as shown in figure 4. Using a stretch stitch on your sewing machine or a 4-thread overlock stitch on your serger, join the pieces right sides together with a ¼″ seam allowance. Do this in the order indicated and mark each "Unit" with a piece of masking tape (or your preferred method), so you can easily identify them in the next step. Don't join the units together until you have all of them finished. Press all your seams to one side.

NOTE: When joining pieces together, be mindful of keeping the maximum stretch of the fabric going in the same direction.

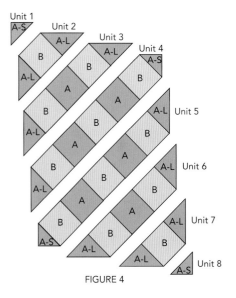

FIGURE 4

4   Once you have all eight units finished, start joining the units, right sides together, with a ¼″ seam allowance. Start with units 1 and 2 on the upper-left

corner and work your way down. Pinning is key in this process to ensure your corner seams are aligned for a professional look. Your quilt top should now look like figure 5. Press all your seams to one side.

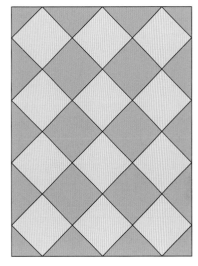

FIGURE 5

5   To assemble your quilt, place the quilt backing (the 2-yard solid piece of fabric you cut at the beginning) over your finished quilt top, right sides together. Trim your quilt backing down to the same size as your top, and then pin the top and backing together all around the outer edges.

OPTIONAL: Since our quilt is made with knit fabrics, which are much thicker and softer than traditional quilting cottons, it's not necessary to add batting, but if you want a warmer, thicker quilt, try adding a layer of cotton quilt batting or fleece between the top and backing. If you decide to add the batting, layer it *on top of the wrong side of your backing* before you cut the corners and stitch (not in between the top and back). This way, it will end up sandwiched inside when you turn the quilt right side out.

6   To round your quilt corners, use a kitchen plate as a template, mark your corners with a fabric-soluble marker (figure 6), then trim all quilt layers together and pin them again.

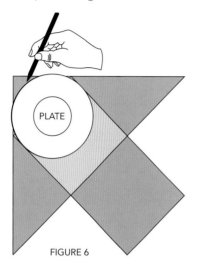

FIGURE 6

7   Stitch the quilt top to the backing ½″ from the raw edges, leaving an 8″ opening on one side for turning. Clip the seam allowances around the curved corners to reduce bulk. Slowly and carefully turn the quilt right side out through the opening, and use your fingers or a blunt tool to make sure all rounded corners are nice and smooth. Press and then topstitch ¼″ from the edge all around, stitching the opening closed.

8   To add flower appliqués to your quilt top, fuse and then stitch the flower centers to each flower first, and then fuse and stitch the flowers to the quilt top. Adhere the appliqués to the quilt top using lightweight fusible web or a quilt basting spray. Use a medium length zigzag stitch on your sewing machine and stitch along the outer edge of the appliqué, making sure the left swing of your zigzag always

penetrates the appliqué while the right swing enters just outside the appliqué's edge into the bottom fabric (figure 7). Stitch slowly around the curved edges. On the sharp points, leave the needle in, lift the presser foot, pivot, lower the presser foot, and continue stitching. Backstitch several times at the end to secure the threads. Clip all the thread tails.

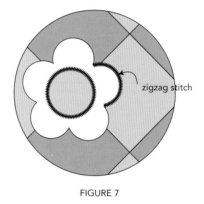

zigzag stitch

FIGURE 7

9   To keep the front and back pieces from shifting around, and also to give your blanket that soft, "quilted" look, sew through all layers using a *Stitch in the Ditch* technique. To Stitch in the Ditch, you use a "walking foot" on your sewing machine to create long, straight lines of quilting along the seams (or "ditches") of the quilt top. Your stitches will be barely visible from the front, and on the back you'll see a ghost image of your quilt top pattern (figure 8).

FRONT (48″ x 65″)   BACK (solid color, quilted stitches)

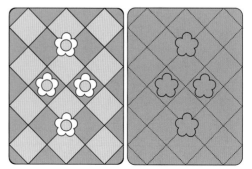

FIGURE 8

Your Harlequin Quilt can be sweet or funky, depending on what fabrics you use. We used a solid cotton interlock paired up with a bold print for our diamond shapes. Then we pulled colors from the print to make our large flowers coordinate perfectly.

CHAPTER 3

bottoms

· · · ·

Om. Sydney reaches a state of total relaxation in her Yoga Pants and Mondrian Shirt (page 97).

yoga pants (or shorts)

NOTES ON FIT: Our Yoga Pants pattern was designed with a snug fit through the waist, hip, and thigh and a slight flare at the hem. The hem hits mid-calf (capri-length). When in doubt, always refer to the sizing chart provided. If you are concerned about it fitting too tightly on the child, you can always go up a size. Also, if you want the pants to be full-length, cut two sizes longer while keeping the width of the pattern to the correct size of the child. Likewise, if you want a shorter fit, cut one or two sizes shorter on the pattern. Every child is unique, so don't be afraid to modify this pattern to fit her perfectly.

double-folded yoga knit waistband

If the terms *sun salutation, downward-facing dog,* and *warrior pose* mean something to you, then you don't need me to tell you about the benefits of yoga for children. But if you've never tried it before, let me just say that yoga not only enhances their flexibility, strength, balance, and coordination, but also helps them reach that state of relaxation and inner peace that all of us need after a busy, hectic day. As with all physical activities, it's important to have the proper attire. Clothing that restricts your child's movement is not suitable for yoga, so these *Yoga Pants (or Shorts)* are perfect because they move and bend with her. Also since they have a non-elastic, double-folded waistband, they won't be tight or uncomfortable around her tummy. Of course, if the yogi lifestyle is not your cup of tea, don't fret; yoga pants make great pajama bottoms and loungewear and are absolutely perfect for traveling. So let's get ready to inhale, exhale, and relax . . . .

Child Sizing Chart			*Finished Yoga Pants Measurements*	
US Size	EURO Size	Child's Height	HIP* CIRCUMFERENCE	LEGGINGS LENGTH*
2T	92	36.25" (92 cm)	21" W	17" L
3T	98	38.75" (98 cm)	22.5" W	18" L
4T	104	41" (104 cm)	23.5" W	19" L
5T	110	43.5" (110 cm)	25" W	20" L
6	116	45" (116 cm)	26" W	21" L
7	122	48" (122 cm)	27.5" W	22.5" L
8/9	128/134	50"-53" (128-134 cm)	29" W	24" L
10	140	55" (140 cm)	30.5" W	25.5" L

*HIP is measured all around. LENGTH assumes a 1/2" hem allowance.
If adding decorative trims that extend past the hem,
please take them into consideration when calculating length.

SUPPLIES

You can use most stretch fabrics for your Yoga Pants (or Shorts) including, but not limited to, cotton interlock, jersey, rib knits, stretch velvet, or stretch velour, 58"/60" wide. Knits with Lycra (spandex) will hold their shape a little better, especially around the knees, and provide more elasticity. Some yogis prefer organic fabrics because of their sustainability and comfort. If this interests you, you can search for organic cotton, bamboo, or hemp knits. Just remember that your yoga waistband needs to have at least a small percentage of Lycra in order to hold up the weight of the pants. Refer to page 10 for more information on types of knits.

Use Pattern Piece A (front and back panel) and Pattern Piece B (waistband) on page 2.

- ¾ yard for sizes 2T–4T OR 1 yard for sizes 5T–10

- Coordinating thread

- Rotary cutter and self-healing mat, or dressmaking shears

- Flexible tape measure for determining your child's waist measurement

CUT

1   Fold the knit fabric in half so the selvedges meet on one side, and cut 2 of Pattern Piece A (front and back panel) and 2 of Pattern Piece B (waistband) on the grain, as shown in figure 1.

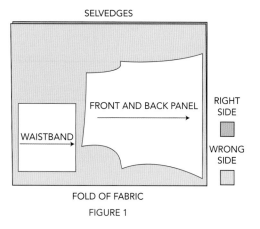

SELVEDGES

FRONT AND BACK PANEL

RIGHT SIDE

WRONG SIDE

WAISTBAND

FOLD OF FABRIC

FIGURE 1

NOTE: If you're concerned about the waistband panel fitting snugly on your child, use this formula to cut your waistband pieces for a perfect fit: Measure your child's waist (all around) using a flexible tape measure. Now, subtract 3″ off that measurement and divide this number by 2 to get the width of each of your 2 non-elastic waistband pieces. (We make these pieces much narrower than the actual waist size because there is no elastic, so the band needs to be taut in order to hold up the weight of the yoga pants.) The height of each panel will be 9″ for any size pants/shorts. *For example: My daughter's waist measures 23″ all around. So, 23″ minus 3″ = 20″ divided by 2 = 10″. I will cut 2 waistband panels at 10″ wide by 9″ tall with the maximum stretch of the fabric running across the 10″ width.*

ASSEMBLE

2   Hem both pant legs while they are flat. To hem, fold up a ½″ hem allowance, press the edge, and then stitch as in figure 2. If you own a coverstitch machine, you can get a very professional finish, although a twin needle on your sewing machine can result in a similar look. Of course, you can always just use a stretch stitch or a zigzag stitch on your sewing machine (see page 26 for hemming techniques for knit fabrics).

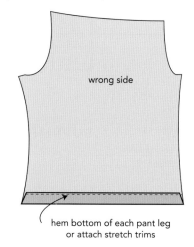

wrong side

hem bottom of each pant leg or attach stretch trims

FIGURE 2

3 Place one pant piece over the other, right sides together, aligning all sides and notches, and then pin. Using a ½″ seam allowance, stitch/serge the front and back center seams as shown in figure 3. If you're not serging the edge, trim the seam allowances down to ¼″ to reduce bulk.

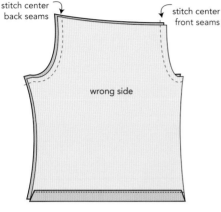

FIGURE 3

4 Now, open up your pants and align the inside leg seams right sides together, matching notches and crotch seams. Pin, then stitch/serge the inseam from one side to the other using a ½″ seam allowance (figure 4). Again, if you're not serging the edge, trim the seam allowances down to ¼″ to reduce bulk. Turn your Yoga Pants (or Shorts) right side out.

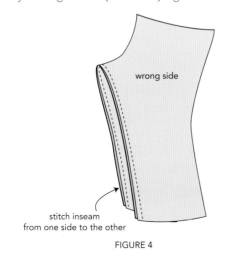

FIGURE 4

5 Now, let's create the yoga waistband by placing one waistband panel over the other, right sides together, and stitching/serging along the side edges (figure 5). Make sure the maximum stretch of the fabric is running side to side so the waistband will stretch nicely over your little one's waist.

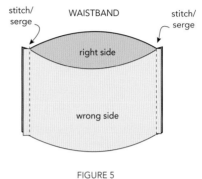

FIGURE 5

6 Fold the waistband panel down in half lengthwise, wrong sides together, encasing both side seams, as shown in figure 6, and press the fold at the top to create a nice crease.

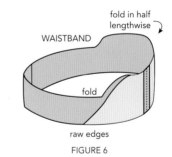

FIGURE 6

7 Attach the waistband to the pants/shorts. Lay your waistband over the right side of the pants' top edge, aligning the seams and keeping the raw edges even.

NOTE: You can choose to align the waistband's side seams with the center seams of the pants or keep them at the sides. If you choose to keep the

Sophie practices her warrior
pose in her comfy and stylish
new Yoga Pants and Mondrian
Shirt (page 97).

waistband seams at the sides, first lay your pants
down on a flat surface and finger-press the sides to
mark the placement of the waistband seams.

8   Pin in place all around, stretching the waistband
slightly to fit. Stitch or serge ½″ from the raw
edges (figure 7). Turn the waistband right side out.
Wear the waistband panel single-layer or double-
folded as preferred.

stitch/serge waistband to pants/shorts

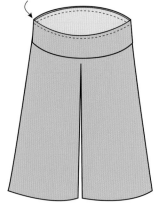

FIGURE 7

The short version of our Yoga Pants is just as comfortable and perfect for outdoor activities and play.

twirly tiered skirt

NOTES ON FIT: Our Twirly Skirt pattern was designed to hit just above the knee. Always refer to the sizing chart provided when in doubt. If you prefer the skirt to be a bit longer, cut the skirt panels one or two sizes longer while keeping the width of the panels to the correct size of the child. Likewise, if you want a shorter skirt, cut your skirt panels one or two sizes shorter. Every child is unique, so don't be afraid to modify this pattern to fit her perfectly.

I have yet to meet a little girl who doesn't love to twirl in a skirt until she gets dizzy. The _Twirly Tiered Skirt_ has three full, gathered panels for maximum twirl power. Comfy and lightweight for summer, it's also perfect as a layering piece for the cooler months. It looks great worn over our Leggings pattern and paired up with any of our cute tops. Make this skirt out of a solid color for a basic wardrobe staple or use three different prints for a funky and whimsical look. Then, dance the night away . . . _at least 'til bedtime!_

Child Sizing Chart			Cutting Guide for Twirly Skirt Pieces		
US Size	EURO Size	SKIRT LENGTH*	1st PANEL CUT 2 PIECES	2nd PANEL CUT 2 PIECES	3rd PANEL CUT 2 PIECES
2T	92	10"	4"h x 12"w	4.5"h x20"w	5"h x 29"w
3T	98	11"	4"h x 12"w	5"h x 20"w	5.5"h x 29"w
4T	104	12"	4"h x 13"w	5.5"h x 21"w	6"h x 32"w
5T	110	13"	4"h x 13"w	6"h x 21"w	6.5"h x 32"w
6	116	14"	4"h x 14"w	6.5"h x 22"w	7"h x 34"w
7	122	15"	4"h x 14"w	7"h x 22"w	7.5"h x 34"w
8/9	128/134	16"	4"h x 15"w	7.5"h x 23"w	8"h x 35"w
10	140	17"	4"h x 16"w	8"h x 24"w	8.5"h x 36"w

*Skirt length assumes a 1/2" hem. Add 1/4" to the finished length if you intend to finish with a rolled hem.

SUPPLIES

You can use most stretch fabrics for your Twirly Skirt including, but not limited to, cotton interlock, jerseys, rib knits, stretch velvet, or stretch velour, 58"/60" wide. Avoid thick fabrics with very little give, like double knits, because they will be harder to gather and bulkier at the seams. Refer to page 10 for more information on types of knits.

No pattern pieces are necessary. Use the cutting guide provided on this page.

- ½ yard of knit fabric for sizes 2T–6 OR ⅔ yard of knit fabric for sizes 7–10
- 18"–22" (depending on size of child) of ½"-wide knit elastic

elastic waistband

Sydney's first day of school outfit was a hit! She wore the Not-So-Plain Tee (page 102) made up in a pre-ruffled jersey and cotton interlock mix, with the Twirly Tiered Skirt layered over a super cute pair of Leggings (page 75) with a pre-ruffle trim at the hem.

- Coordinating thread

- Rotary cutter and self-healing mat, or dressmaking shears

- Flexible tape measure for determining your child's waist measurement

- **OPTIONAL:** stretch trims (stretch lace, stretch ribbon, knit ruffles, and so on) to embellish skirt hem

CUT

Refer to the cutting guide provided on the previous page to determine what size to cut each skirt panel. Remember that the maximum stretch of the fabric should always go side-to-side (along the longest of the measurements) on these panels. You should have six skirt panels, two of each size.

Cut a piece of ½″ knit elastic exactly 1″ shorter than the waist measurement of the child. If you don't have a child to measure, use the chart below for an approximate measure:

Sizes 2T and 3T = 16″ long

Sizes 4T and 5 = 18″ long

Sizes 6 and 7 = 20″ long

Sizes 8/9 and 10 = 22″ long

If using stretch trims to embellish the hems, cut 2 equal pieces just slightly longer than the width of the skirt hem (the widest of the panels) for the size of skirt you are making.

ASSEMBLE

1   Take the two smallest skirt panels, which we will refer to as the waistband panels, and place them right sides together. Pin, then stitch/serge along the two short sides, creating a circular band (figure 1).

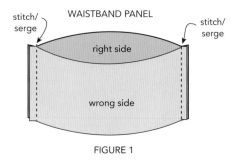

FIGURE 1

2   Create an elastic casing at the top of your waistband panel by folding the edge down ¼″ toward the wrong side, pressing, then folding again another ¾″. Stitch near the lower folded edge but leave a 1″–2″ gap on the center back for inserting the elastic (figure 2). *Don't insert the elastic yet.* It's much easier to do this as a last step, after the skirt is completely sewn together.

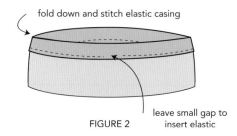

FIGURE 2

3   Repeat step 1 with the other two sets of skirt panels. You should now have three circular bands of ascending sizes, one with a waistband casing and two without. We will call the mid-size band panel #2, and the largest band panel #3 (figure 3).

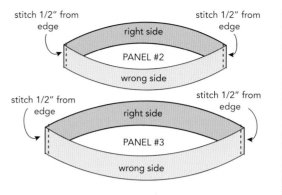

stitch 1/2" from edge

stitch 1/2" from edge

right side

PANEL #2

wrong side

stitch 1/2" from edge

stitch 1/2" from edge

right side

PANEL #3

wrong side

FIGURE 3

4   Now it's time to gather the two skirt panels. Begin by running two lines of long, gathering stitches along the top edge of each skirt panel. The first row should be ⅛" from the top edge and the second row should be just ⅛" below the first. *Don't backstitch at the end.* You need those threads loose so you can grab and pull. Now using your fingers, grab the bobbin threads and carefully pull to gather the top edge of panel #2 to the same width as the waistband panel. Likewise, gather the top of panel #3 to the same width as the bottom of panel #2 (figure 4).

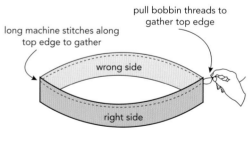

long machine stitches along top edge to gather

pull bobbin threads to gather top edge

wrong side

right side

FIGURE 4

5   Attach panel #2 to the waistband panel by placing the two panels right sides together so that the gathered edge of panel #2 is even with the bottom raw edge of the waistband panel. Make

sure both side seams are aligned, and place a pin on each side to prevent them from shifting. Pin all around, then stitch/serge the edges together with a ½" seam allowance (figure 5). If you're serging, the blades of your serger will automatically trim off the gathered edge, but if you're using a sewing machine, make sure you trim the seams down or remove the gathering stitches with a seam ripper.

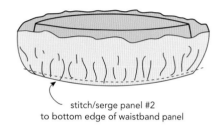

stitch/serge panel #2 to bottom edge of waistband panel

FIGURE 5

6   Attach panel #3 to the bottom of panel #2 in the same manner that you did in step 5 (figure 6). Press all your seams down.

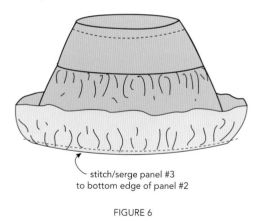

stitch/serge panel #3 to bottom edge of panel #2

FIGURE 6

7   Finish the bottom edge of the skirt with your preferred hemming method. See page 26 for a list of hemming techniques for knit fabrics. If you decide to attach a trim, like stretch lace, ribbon, or ruffles, to the skirt bottom, it is not necessary to hem first.

Use a large safety pin or a bodkin to help guide the elastic into the waistband casing you created in step 2 (figure 7).

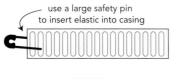

use a large safety pin to insert elastic into casing

FIGURE 7

8 Pull the end of the elastic out through the gap, overlap the ends, and then stitch them together, as shown in figure 8. Try the skirt on your child to ensure a good fit, once the waistband is nice and snug, stitch the gap closed and you're done!

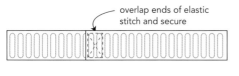

overlap ends of elastic stitch and secure

FIGURE 8

TIP: To keep the elastic from twisting and turning inside the waist casing (yes, even the so-called "non-roll elastic" will do that over time), run a row of vertical stitches along the side seams of the casing, stitching right through the elastic and backstitching at the ends to secure the threads.

Whether you use one fabric print, several prints, or bring solids into the mix, our Twirly Tiered Skirt always looks fabulous.

bubble skirt

NOTES ON FIT: Our Bubble Skirt pattern was designed to hit right at the knee with a drop-waist design. This means the "bubble" part of the skirt begins at the hip—not at the waist. Always refer to the sizing chart provided when in doubt. Every child is unique, so don't be afraid to modify this pattern to fit her perfectly.

Our *Bubble Skirt* is a quick and easy project that will be a hit among little girls. It adds an extra bit of pizzazz to even the plainest of outfits and goes perfectly with all of our Modkid tops. Wear it in the winter over a pair of tights or in the summer with a cute pair of sandals, and let her bubbly personality shine through.

Child Sizing Chart			*Finished Bubble Skirt Measurements*	
US Size	EURO Size	Child's Height	WAIST* CIRCUMFERENCE	BUBBLE SKIRT LENGTH
2T	92	36.25" (92 cm)	16" W	11.75" L
3T	98	38.75" (98 cm)	16" W	12.0" L
4T	104	41" (104 cm)	18" W	12.25" L
5T	110	43.5" (110 cm)	18" W	12.5" L
6	116	45" (116 cm)	20" W	12.75" L
7	122	48" (122 cm)	20" W	13.0" L
8/9	128/134	50"-53" (128-134 cm)	22" W	13.25" L
10	140	55" (140 cm)	22" W	13.5" L

*WAIST is measured all around and can be adjusted to the child's measurements.

SUPPLIES

You can use most stretch fabrics for your Bubble Skirt including, but not limited to, cotton interlock, jerseys, double knits, rib knits, stretch velvet, or stretch velour, 58"/60" wide. Refer to page 10 for more information on types of knits.

Use Pattern Pieces D (inner skirt) and B (waistband) on page 3.

There are no pattern pieces for the outer skirt; use the chart on page 71 to cut your panels.

- 1 yard of knit fabric
- ½–¾ yard (depending on size of child) of ½"-wide knit elastic
- Coordinating thread
- Rotary cutter, straightedge ruler, and self-healing mat; or dressmaking shears

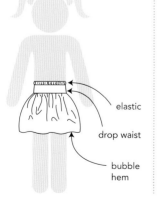

elastic

drop waist

bubble hem

Our sweet Bubble Skirt dresses up
any plain knit top with such pizzazz.

- Flexible tape measure for determining your child's size

CUT

Cut 2 waistbands and 2 inner skirts, as shown in figure 1. Cut 2 outer skirt panels using the chart below (maximum stretch of fabric running across the width). Make sure you use a knit fabric with plenty of body for the skirt. Thin or slinky knits will not give it that "bubble" effect.

For the outer skirt:

Size 2T = 2 panels, 11″ high × 25½″ wide each

Size 3T = 2 panels, 11½″ high × 26″ wide each

Size 4T = 2 panels, 12″ high × 26½″ wide each

Size 5T = 2 panels, 12½″ high × 27″ wide each

Size 6 = 2 panels, 13″ high × 27½″ wide each

Size 7 = 2 panels, 13½″ high × 28″ wide each

Size 8/9 = 2 panels, 14″ high × 28½″ wide each

Size 10 = 2 panels, 14½″ high × 29″ wide each

Cut a piece of ½″ knit elastic exactly 1″ shorter than the waist measurement of the child, or use the chart below for an approximate measure:

Sizes 2T and 3T = 16″ long

Sizes 4T and 5 = 18″ long

Sizes 6 and 7 = 20″ long

Sizes 8/9 and 10 = 22″ long

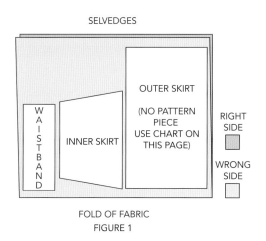

SELVEDGES

WAISTBAND

INNER SKIRT

OUTER SKIRT

(NO PATTERN PIECE USE CHART ON THIS PAGE)

RIGHT SIDE

WRONG SIDE

FOLD OF FABRIC
FIGURE 1

ASSEMBLE

1   With right sides together, pin and then stitch/serge along both side seams of your inner skirt using a ½″ seam allowance (figure 2). Turn right side out.

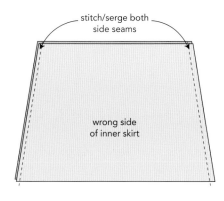

stitch/serge both side seams

wrong side of inner skirt

FIGURE 2

2   With right sides together, pin and then stitch/serge along both side seams of your outer skirt using a ½″ seam allowance (figure 3). Turn right side out.

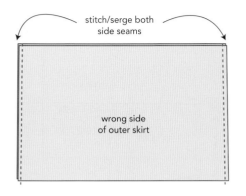

stitch/serge both side seams

wrong side
of outer skirt

FIGURE 3

3   Gather the top and bottom edges of the outer skirt. Run a couple of long machine stitches along the top and bottom edges, and then gently pull the bobbin threads to gather the fabric. Use your fingers to evenly distribute the folds. Gather the top edge to the width of the inner skirt's top edge. Gather the bottom edge to the width of the inner skirt's bottom edge (figure 4).

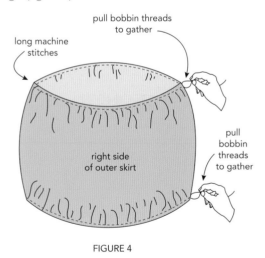

long machine
stitches

pull bobbin threads
to gather

pull
bobbin
threads
to gather

right side
of outer skirt

FIGURE 4

4   Turn the outer skirt inside out, but leave the inner skirt right side out. Insert the inner skirt inside the outer skirt (figure 5).

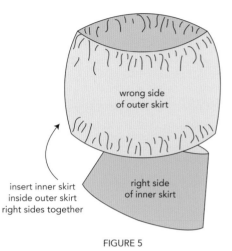

wrong side
of outer skirt

insert inner skirt
inside outer skirt
right sides together

right side
of inner skirt

FIGURE 5

5   Quarter-mark the bottom edges of both skirts to ensure the gathers are evenly distributed and side seams are aligned. Pin, then stitch/serge them together with a ½″ seam allowance (figure 6). *Don't sew the top edges yet!*

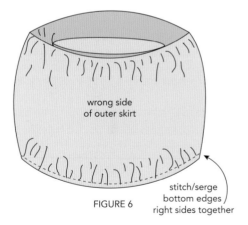

wrong side
of outer skirt

stitch/serge
bottom edges
right sides together

FIGURE 6

6   Turn your entire skirt right side out (outer skirt on the outside) so the wrong sides are facing on your skirts. Align the side seams, quarter-mark, and pin the top edges together. Baste (figure 7).

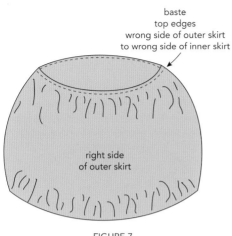

baste
top edges
wrong side of outer skirt
to wrong side of inner skirt

right side
of outer skirt

FIGURE 7

7 Now, let's create the drop waistband by placing one waistband panel over the other, right sides together, and stitching/serging along the side edges (figure 8). Make sure the maximum stretch of the fabric is running side to side so the waistband will stretch nicely over your little one's waist.

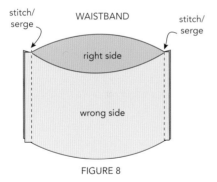

stitch/
serge

WAISTBAND

stitch/
serge

right side

wrong side

FIGURE 8

8 Fold the waistband panel down in half lengthwise, wrong sides together, encasing both side seams, as shown in figure 9. Press the fold at the top to create a nice crease.

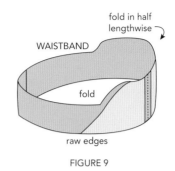

fold in half
lengthwise

WAISTBAND

fold

raw edges

FIGURE 9

9 Create a casing for the elastic by stitching ⅝″ from the folded edge. Leave a 2″ gap in the center back for inserting the elastic (figure 10).

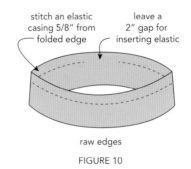

stitch an elastic
casing 5/8″ from
folded edge

leave a
2″ gap for
inserting elastic

raw edges

FIGURE 10

10 Use a large safety pin or a bodkin to help guide the elastic into the casing you just created (figure 11).

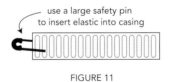

use a large safety pin
to insert elastic into casing

FIGURE 11

11 Pull the end of the elastic out through the gap, overlap the ends, and then stitch them together as shown in figure 12. Stitch the opening closed.

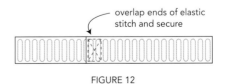

overlap ends of elastic
stitch and secure

FIGURE 12

12 Attach the waistband to the bubble skirt. Lay your waistband over the right side of the skirt's top edge, aligning the side seams and keeping the raw edges even. Pin in place all around, stretching the waistband slightly to fit. Stitch or serge ½" from the raw edges (figure 13). Turn the waistband right side out.

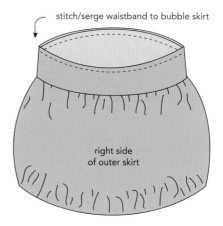

stitch/serge waistband to bubble skirt

right side
of outer skirt

FIGURE 13

Sweet and casual for a summer day excursion, Sydney's Bubble Skirt is made of Raspberry Blossoms and Clown Stripes cotton interlock.

leggings

What's cuter than a pair of bright-colored leggings under a twirly skirt or dress? Nope, it's not a trick question. The answer is nothing! I love making these since they're so quick and easy and don't use up a lot of fabric. *Leggings* **are quite practical as** they can be used to keep little legs warm on chilly winter days, yet they're a lot of fun as a fashion statement. They can dress an outfit up or down. And depending on the fabric and trims you use, they can say classy, funky, or sweet. So let's kick the cuteness up a notch and make some leggings!

NOTES ON FIT: We designed the Leggings pattern to be worn under clothes, so it has a snug fit to reduce bulk and the hem hits mid-calf. Always refer to the sizing chart provided when in doubt. If you are concerned about it fitting too tightly on the child, you can always go up a size. Also, if you want the leggings to be full-length, cut one or two sizes longer while keeping the width of the pattern to the correct size of the child. Likewise, if you want a shorter legging, cut one or two sizes shorter on the pattern. Every child is unique, so don't be afraid to modify this pattern to fit her perfectly.

Child Sizing Chart			Finished Leggings Measurements	
US Size	EURO Size	Child's Height	HIP* CIRCUMFERENCE	LEGGINGS LENGTH*
2T	92	36.25" (92 cm)	21" W	17" L
3T	98	38.75" (98 cm)	22.5" W	18" L
4T	104	41" (104 cm)	23.5" W	19" L
5T	110	43.5" (110 cm)	25" W	20" L
6	116	45" (116 cm)	26" W	21" L
7	122	48" (122 cm)	27.5" W	22.5" L
8/9	128/134	50"-53" (128-134 cm)	29" W	24" L
10	140	55" (140 cm)	30.5" W	25.5" L

*HIP is measured all around. LENGTH assumes a 1/2" hem allowance.
If adding decorative trims that extend past the hem,
please take them into consideration when calculating length.

SUPPLIES

You can use most stretch fabrics for your leggings including, but not limited to, cotton interlock, jersey, rib knits, stretch velvet, or stretch velour, 58"/60" wide. Knits with a small percentage of Lycra (spandex) will hold their shape a little better, especially around the knees. If you make these leggings out of a Nylon/Lycra blend, they will be perfect for dancewear. Refer to page 10 for more information on types of knits.

Use Pattern Piece A on page 1.

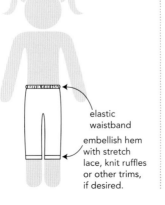

elastic waistband

embellish hem with stretch lace, knit ruffles or other trims, if desired.

BFFs Sydney and Anna pair their leggings with their Tie Strap Halter (page 92) and Twirly Tiered Skirt (page 64) for a complete boutique-style ensemble.

- ⅔ yard for sizes 2T–6, ¾ yard for sizes 7 and 8/9, OR 1 yard for size 10
- 18″–22″ (depending on size of child) of ½″-wide knit elastic
- Coordinating thread
- Rotary cutter and self-healing mat, or dressmaking shears
- Flexible tape measure for determining your child's waist measurement
- **OPTIONAL:** stretch trims (stretch lace, stretch ribbon, knit ruffles, and so on) to embellish hems

CUT

Fold the knit fabric in half so the selvedges meet, and cut 2 of Pattern Piece A on the grain as shown in figure 1.

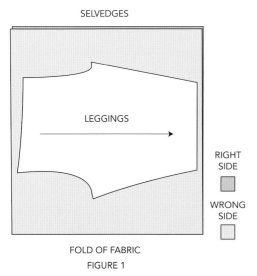

SELVEDGES

LEGGINGS

RIGHT SIDE

WRONG SIDE

FOLD OF FABRIC

FIGURE 1

Cut a piece of ½″ knit elastic exactly 1″ shorter than the waist measurement of the child. If you don't have a child to measure, use the following chart for an approximate measure:

Sizes 2T and 3T = 16″ long

Sizes 4T and 5 = 18″ long

Sizes 6 and 7 = 20″ long

Sizes 8/9 and 10 = 22″ long

If using stretch trims to embellish the hems, cut 2 equal pieces just slightly longer than the width of the hem for the size of leggings you are making.

ASSEMBLE

1   If attaching stretch trims to your leggings' hem, do this now while they are still flat. You can stitch them right on to the raw edge with a zigzag stitch on your sewing machine or an overlock serger. Stretch the trims slightly as you attach them to the leggings so they will contract later and hug the leg for a better fit.

NOTE: It is important to use a stretch stitch when attaching trims so the threads won't snap as the legging stretches over the foot.

2   If you're not attaching trims, go ahead and hem both pant legs while they are flat, since the opening will be too narrow to hem after they are sewn together. To hem, fold up a ½″ hem allowance, press the edge, and then stitch as shown in figure 2. If you own a coverstitch machine, you can get a very professional finish, although a twin needle on your sewing machine can result in a similar look. Of course, you can always just use a stretch stitch or a zigzag stitch on your sewing machine (see page 26 for hemming techniques for knit fabrics).

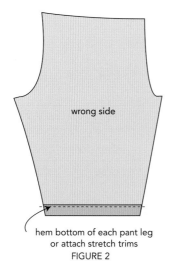

hem bottom of each pant leg
or attach stretch trims
FIGURE 2

3 Place one legging piece over the other right sides together, aligning all sides and notches, and then pin. Using a ½″ seam allowance, stitch/serge the front and back center seams as shown in figure 3. If you're not serging the edge, trim the seam allowances down to ¼″ to reduce bulk.

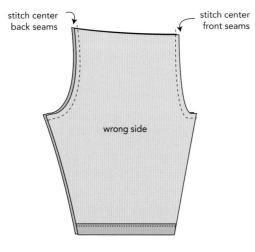

stitch center back seams

stitch center front seams

wrong side

FIGURE 3

4 Now, open up your leggings and align the inside leg seams right sides together, matching notches and crotch seams. Pin, then stitch/serge the

inseam from one side to the other using a ½″ seam allowance (figure 4). Again, if you're not serging the edge, trim the seam allowances down to ¼″ to reduce bulk.

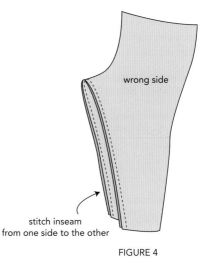

wrong side

stitch inseam
from one side to the other
FIGURE 4

5 Create an elastic casing at the waist of your leggings by folding the edge down ¼″ toward the wrong side, pressing, and then folding again another ¾″. Stitch near the lower folded edge but leave a 1″–2″ gap on the center back for inserting the elastic (figure 5).

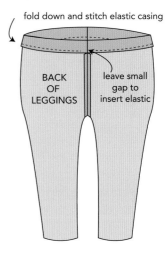

fold down and stitch elastic casing

BACK
OF
LEGGINGS

leave small
gap to
insert elastic

FIGURE 5

6 Use a large safety pin or a bodkin to help guide the elastic into the casing you just created (figure 6).

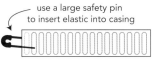

use a large safety pin
to insert elastic into casing

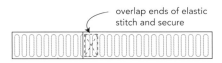

FIGURE 6

7 Pull the end of the elastic out through the gap, overlap the ends, and then stitch them together, as shown in figure 7. Try the leggings on your child to ensure a good fit; once the waistband is nice and snug, stitch the gap closed and you're done!

overlap ends of elastic
stitch and secure

FIGURE 7

Get creative with stretch trims! We've used stretch lace, stretch ribbon, picot-edge elastic, and organza trims to hem our leggings, but a simple turned up and topstitched hem is also perfect.

We achieved the look of "skinny jeans" or "jeggings" by using a denim knit on Sophie's leggings. We topstitched all the seams with a coverstitch (but you can achieve the same effect with a twin needle on your sewing machine), and we even added a faux seam running vertically down the side of the leggings to simulate the look of jeans.

TIP: To keep the elastic from twisting and turning inside the waist casing (yes, even the so-called "non-roll elastic" will do that over time), run a row of vertical stitches along the center front seam and center back seam of the casing, stitching right through the elastic and backstitching at the ends to secure the threads.

Sydney strikes a pose in her fun and funky A-Line Gored Skirt paired up with an adorable Mondrian Shirt (page 97).

A-line gored skirt

NOTES ON FIT: Our A-Line Gored Skirt pattern was designed to hit right above the knee with the 4″ waistband panel worn single-layer, not double-folded. Always refer to the sizing chart provided when in doubt. If you want a longer skirt, cut the length of the gores one or two sizes longer while keeping the width of the gores to the correct size of the child. Likewise, if you want a shorter skirt, cut your gores one or two sizes shorter. Every child is unique, so don't be afraid to modify this pattern to fit her perfectly.

A modern twist on a vintage style, our *A-Line Gored Skirt* is super sassy with its swingy silhouette and clean lines. Girls will love how comfy it is with its non-elastic yoga waistband—just pull on and go. And you'll love how quickly and easily it goes together.

Use many prints for a funky look or make it out of one or two fabric designs for a classier look. It looks great over leggings and paired up with any of our tops.

Child Sizing Chart			*Finished A-line Skirt Measurements*	
US Size	EURO Size	Child's Height	HIP* CIRCUMFERENCE	SKIRT LENGTH*
2T	92	36.25″ (92 cm)	21″ W	12.75″ L
3T	98	38.75″ (98 cm)	22.5″ W	13.25″ L
4T	104	41″ (104 cm)	23.5″ W	14″ L
5T	110	43.5″ (110 cm)	25″ W	14.5″ L
6	116	45″ (116 cm)	26″ W	15″ L
7	122	48″ (122 cm)	27.5″ W	15.75″ L
8/9	128/134	50″-53″ (128-134 cm)	29″ W	16.5″ L
10	140	55″ (140 cm)	30.5″ W	17.25″ L

*HIP is measured all around. LENGTH includes a 4″ waistband. Waist size is determined by user and cut to size.

SUPPLIES

You can use most stretch fabrics for your A-Line Gored Skirt including, but not limited to, cotton interlock, jerseys, double knits, rib knits, stretch velvet, or stretch velour, 58″/60″ wide. We like to use rib knits or other fabrics with Lycra (spandex) content for the non-elastic waistband panel, because they hug the waist better due to their great recovery and will stay snug through many uses. Refer to page 10 for more information on types of knits.

Use Pattern Pieces A (gores) on page 3 and B (waistband) on page 2, or create your own snug waistband panel with our easy instructions.

- 1 yard of knit fabric (or use remnants of different fabric prints for a funky look)
- Coordinating thread

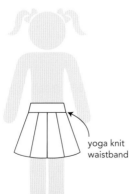

yoga knit waistband

- Rotary cutter, straightedge ruler, and self-healing mat; or dressmaking shears
- Flexible tape measure for determining your child's size

CUT

Cut 8 gores and 2 waistband panels as shown in figure 1. If your fabric has a directional print, place your pattern pieces as indicated on the left-side diagram, but if you're using non-directional fabrics, maximize space by placing them as shown on the right-side diagram. Of course, don't be afraid to get creative with fabrics and use all those remnants in your studio. Just remember to always keep the maximum stretch of the fabrics going side-to-side on those gores so the skirt will drape better.

FOR DIRECTIONAL PRINTS, ALWAYS PLACE PATTERN PIECES LIKE THIS:

NON-DIRECTIONAL FABRICS CAN BE CUT LIKE THIS:

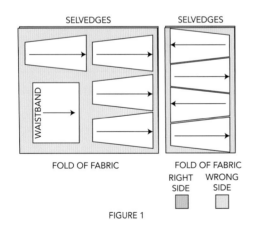

FIGURE 1

NOTE: If you're concerned about the waistband panel fitting snugly on your child, use this formula to cut your waistband pieces for a perfect fit: Measure your child's waist (all around) using a flexible tape measure. Now, subtract 3″ off that measurement and divide this number by 2 to get the width of each of your 2 non-elastic waistband pieces. (We make these pieces much narrower than the actual waist size because there is no elastic, so the band needs to be taut in order to hold up the weight of the skirt.) The height of each panel will be 9″ for any size skirt. *For example: My daughter's waist measures 23″ all around. So, 23″ minus 3″ = 20″ divided by 2 = 10″. I will cut 2 waistband panels at 10″ wide by 9″ tall with the maximum stretch of the fabric running across the 10″ width.*

ASSEMBLE

1 Begin by laying out your eight gore pieces on your sewing table in the order you want them to appear on your skirt. Now take the first and second gore and stitch/serge them together along one side edge, right sides together, with a ½″ seam allowance (figure 2). Press the seam open if not serging, or to one side if serging.

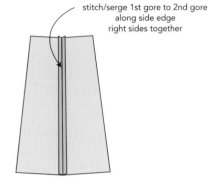

stitch/serge 1st gore to 2nd gore along side edge right sides together

FIGURE 2

2 Stitch/serge the remainder of the gores in the same fashion until you have all eight gores stitched together in a row (figure 3).

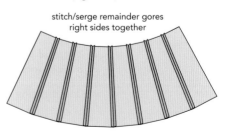

stitch/serge remainder gores right sides together

FIGURE 3

3 Fold the skirt in half, right sides together, and close up the sides by stitching/serging the first gore to the last along the side edge (figure 4). Turn right side out.

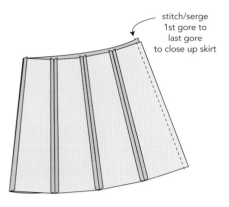

FIGURE 4

4 Now, let's create the yoga waistband by placing one waistband panel over the other, right sides together, and stitching/serging along the side edges (figure 5). Make sure the maximum stretch of the fabric is running side to side so the waistband will stretch nicely over your little one's waist.

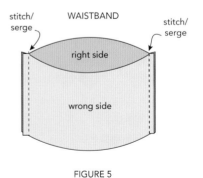

FIGURE 5

5 Fold the waistband panel down in half lengthwise, wrong sides together, encasing both side seams, as shown in figure 6, and press the fold at the top to create a nice crease.

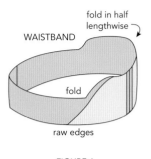

FIGURE 6

6 Attach the waistband to the skirt. Lay your waistband over the right side of the skirt's top edge, aligning the side seams and keeping the raw edges even. There should be four gores in the front and four gores in the back. Pin in place all around, stretching the waistband slightly to fit. (Your waistband panel will naturally be narrower than the skirt.) Stitch/serge ½″ from the raw edges (figure 7). Turn the waistband right side out.

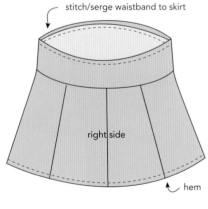

FIGURE 7

7 Hem the skirt as desired. See page 26 for hemming techniques with knits. Wear the waistband panel single-layer or double-folded as preferred.

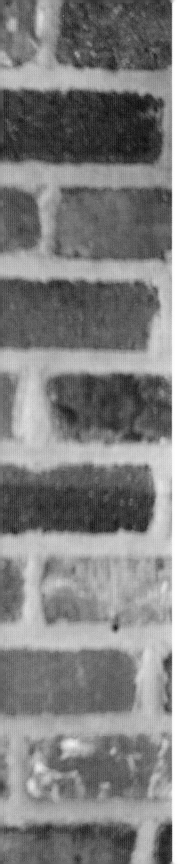

CHAPTER 4

tops

• • • •

How snazzy is this size 10 Banded Tank Top for your 10-going-on-16 girl?! We used this super funky Mod Waves cotton jersey and paired it up with a solid black cotton interlock for a sophisticated, yet playful look.

banded tank top

NOTES ON FIT: Our Banded Tank Top was designed to fit snugly across the chest and hips with a "bubble" look in the middle. The hem hits right at the hips, but can also be worn higher up for a "bubblier" look.

Show off her bubbly personality with this sweet *Banded Tank Top*. If you have a bright, bold fabric print that you've been saving for a special project, this is the perfect top for that. Comfy and lightweight for the summer months or layered over a long-sleeve tee for the cooler months, this top will soon become a wardrobe fave. Pair it up with our Yoga Pants or any of our cute skirts for a look that will turn heads.

Child Sizing Chart			Finished Tank Measurements	
US Size	EURO Size	Child's Height	CHEST* CIRCUMFERENCE	HALTER LENGTH*
2T	92	36.25" (92 cm)	19.5" W	16" L
3T	98	38.75" (98 cm)	20" W	17" L
4T	104	41" (104 cm)	20.5" W	18" L
5T	110	43.5" (110 cm)	21" W	19" L
6	116	45" (116 cm)	21.5" W	20" L
7	122	48" (122 cm)	22" W	21" L
8/9	128/134	50"-53" (128-134 cm)	23" W	22" L
10	140	55" (140 cm)	24" W	23" L

*CHEST is measured all around. LENGTH is measured from shoulder to hem.

SUPPLIES

You can use most stretch fabrics for your banded top including, but not limited to, cotton interlock, matte jerseys, double knits, rib knits, stretch velvet, or stretch velour, 58"/60" wide. We like to use rib knits or other fabrics with Lycra (spandex) content for the top band, bottom band, and shoulder straps, because they have great structure and will hold their shape through many uses. Refer to page 10 for more information on types of knits.

Use Pattern Piece A (top band), B (center panel), C (bottom band), and D (shoulder straps) on page 4.

- For the contrast bands (top, bottom, and shoulder straps) ⅓ yard of rib knit or other knit fabric with Lycra content

- For the main tank top panel, ¼ yard for size 2T, ⅓ yard for sizes 3T–8/9, and ½ yard for size 10.
- Coordinating thread
- Two decorative buttons (no larger than ½" diameter) as desired
- Rotary cutter and self-healing mat, or dressmaking shears

CUT

Fold your main knit fabric in half so the selvedges meet on one side, and cut 1 center panel on the fold as shown in figure 1. Fold the coordinating rib knit (or similar fabric) so the selvedges meet in the middle, and cut 2 top bands on the fold, 1 bottom band on the fold, and 2 shoulder straps as shown in figure 1.

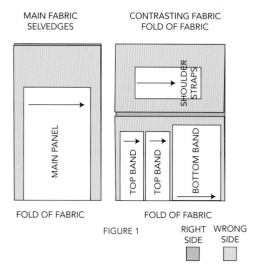

FIGURE 1

RIGHT SIDE   WRONG SIDE

ASSEMBLE

1   Assemble both shoulder straps first by folding them right sides together lengthwise and stitching/serging the sides closed to form a long, narrow tube. Use your preferred turning tool to turn the straps right side out, and press them flat so that the seam is centered in the back (figure 2).

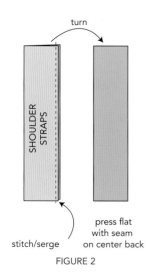

FIGURE 2

2   Fold both top bands in half, right sides together, as shown in figure 3, and stitch/serge them along the short sides to form two circular bands. Press the seams flat. *Don't join the bands together yet.*

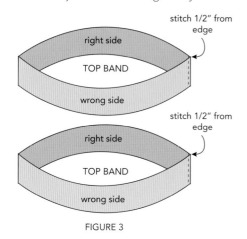

FIGURE 3

3   Turn one of the top bands right side out and finger-press the center front, while the seam is centered in the back. Measure 1½" for sizes 2T–5T or 2" for sizes 6–10 from the center front to the left and right, and mark the spot with a pin or a fabric marker. Do the same on the back of the band. With the shoulder straps' seams facing outward, pin the short ends of the shoulder straps onto the front of the top band as shown in figure 4. Baste both shoulder straps to the front, making sure you have 3″ to 4″ of space in between them, depending on the size (figure 4). Then fold the straps under the top band and baste the other short ends to the back of the band. You will be basting the straps to the band right sides together (figure 5).

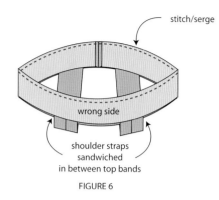

FIGURE 6

5   Turn the entire top piece right side out. Gently tug on the shoulder straps to make sure they are pulled out all the way, and then press all the seams flat. Hand-stitch a couple of decorative buttons at the center front, hiding your stitches in between the top band layers (figure 7). This protects your child's sensitive skin from itchy spots.

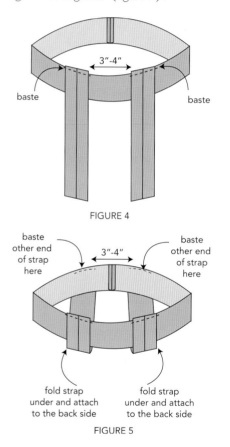

FIGURE 4

FIGURE 5

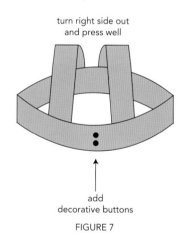

FIGURE 7

4   Once both shoulder straps are secured in place, place the second top band over the first one right sides together, sandwiching the shoulder straps in between the bands, as shown in figure 6. Make sure the back seams are aligned. Stitch/serge all along the top edge with a ½″ seam allowance.

6   To create the bottom band, fold the band right sides together widthwise, as shown in figure 8, and then stitch/serge the short sides closed, creating a circular band. Fold the band in half lengthwise, encasing the seam, and press the folded edge. Set the bottom band aside for now.

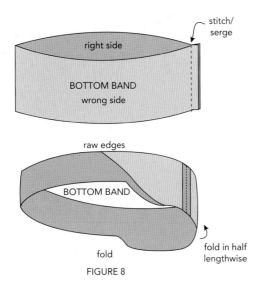

FIGURE 8

7 Create the center panel by folding the panel right sides together widthwise, as shown in figure 9, and then stitching/serging the short sides closed, creating a circular band.

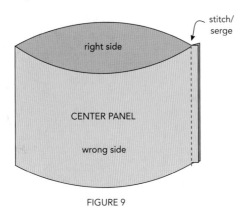

FIGURE 9

8 Run two lines of long machine stitches close to the top and bottom edges of the center panel, and gently pull on the bobbin threads to gather the edges to roughly the same width as the finished top and bottom bands of the shirt (figure 10).

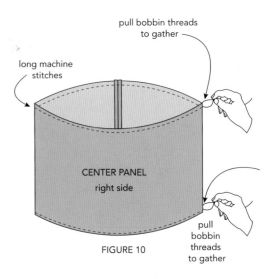

FIGURE 10

9 Make sure all center back seams are perfectly aligned, and then pin the center panel to the top and bottom bands, right sides together, using your fingers to evenly distribute the gathered fabric as needed. Stitch/serge the center panel to the raw edges of the top and bottom bands (figure 11). When finished, turn it right side out, and press all seams toward the bottom.

TIP: If you're using a serger, the serger blades will trim off the gathering stitches on the center panel, but if you're using a sewing machine, go ahead and remove the rows of gathering stitches with a seam ripper, so that the center panel will stretch as needed. Always remember to use a stretch stitch when sewing knits.

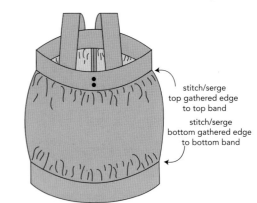

FIGURE 11

Sydney's Banded Tank Top is made with Michael Miller's Scandi Chirp cotton interlock and a coordinating solid rib knit. How perfect is this top?!

Whether you use a bold print or a simple solid, our Tie Strap Halter always looks sweet.

tie strap halter

NOTES ON FIT: Our Tie Strap Halter pattern was designed with a snug fit, and the hem band hits just below the waist. Always refer to the sizing chart provided when in doubt. If you are concerned about this garment fitting too tightly on the child, you can always go up a size. Also, if you prefer a longer top, cut one or two sizes longer while keeping the width of the pattern to the correct size of the child. Every child is unique, so don't be afraid to modify this pattern to fit her perfectly.

The *Tie Strap Halter* has been a summer wardrobe staple at our home for years. I've made this style of top for my girls since they were toddlers, and as they grow older, it's still a favorite around here with just some basic fabric changes. Pair this adorable top with any of the skirts, pants, or leggings in this book for a complete boutique-style ensemble. For some pop, add some fun accessories, like our Rosy Headband or our lightweight Stripwork Scarf, and she will make a fashion statement anywhere she goes.

Child Sizing Chart			Finished Halter Measurements	
US Size	EURO Size	Child's Height	CHEST* CIRCUMFERENCE	HALTER LENGTH*
2T	92	36.25" (92 cm)	19.5" W	15" L
3T	98	38.75" (98 cm)	20" W	16" L
4T	104	41" (104 cm)	20.5" W	17" L
5T	110	43.5" (110 cm)	21" W	18" L
6	116	45" (116 cm)	21.5" W	19" L
7	122	48" (122 cm)	22" W	20" L
8/9	128/134	50"-53" (128-134 cm)	23" W	21" L
10	140	55" (140 cm)	24" W	22" L

*CHEST is measured all around. LENGTH is measured from shoulder to hem.

SUPPLIES

You can use most stretch fabrics for your halter top including, but not limited to, cotton interlock, matte jerseys, double knits, rib knits, stretch velvet, or stretch velour, 58"/60" wide.

Use Pattern Pieces A (front panel), B (front facing), C (back panel), and D (hem band) on page 5.

- ⅔ yard for sizes 2T–6, ¾ yard for sizes 7 and 8/9, OR 1 yard for size 10
- If you desire a contrast bottom band as shown in our samples, you'll need ⅙ yard (or 5 linear inches) of contrast fabric. The remainder required yardage is for the main halter pieces.

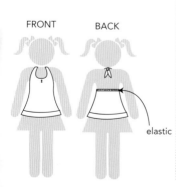

FRONT   BACK

elastic

- 9"–12" (depending on child's size) of ½"-wide knit elastic
- Coordinating thread
- Two or three decorative buttons (no larger than ½" diameter) as desired
- Rotary cutter and self-healing mat, or dressmaking shears
- Flexible tape measure for determining your child's measurements

CUT

Fold the knit fabric so the selvedges meet in the middle, and cut Pattern Pieces A, B, C, and D as shown in figure 1. We like to use a coordinating fabric for the front facing (B) and hem band (D) to add a pop of color. When you use a different color for the facing than the rest of the top, it shows when you tie the straps in the back and looks super cute.

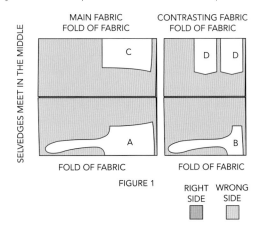

MAIN FABRIC
FOLD OF FABRIC

CONTRASTING FABRIC
FOLD OF FABRIC

SELVEDGES MEET IN THE MIDDLE

C

D D

A

B

FOLD OF FABRIC

FOLD OF FABRIC

FIGURE 1

RIGHT SIDE   WRONG SIDE

Cut a piece of ½" elastic according to the guide provided below:

Sizes 2T and 3T = 8" long

Sizes 4T and 5 = 9" long

Sizes 6 and 7 = 10" long

Sizes 8/9 and 10 = 11" long

If you're concerned about the right fit, you can measure the child's back from side to side to get a more accurate measure.

ASSEMBLE

1   Finish the bottom edge of the front facing piece with an overlock serger or a zigzag stitch on your sewing machine (figure 2).

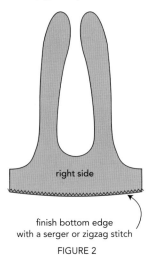

right side

finish bottom edge
with a serger or zigzag stitch

FIGURE 2

2   Place the facing over the front bodice piece right sides together, and pin all around. Using a ½" seam allowance, stitch all along the top from the left side to the right, leaving the sides and bottom edges unstitched, as shown in figure 3. It's best to use a stretch or a small zigzag stitch on your sewing machine and stitch slowly around the straps to get a smooth curve. Trim the seam allowances down to reduce bulk and clip around the curved edges, then turn the bodice right side out and press flat. Baste along the side edges (figure 4).

TIP: Use a blunt tool like a bamboo creaser or the wide end of a wooden chopstick to push the fabric on your straps all the way out.

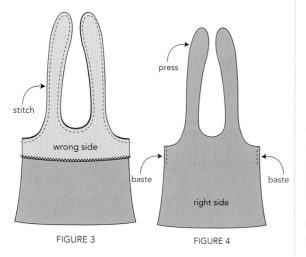

FIGURE 3

FIGURE 4

3 Create an elastic casing at the top of your back piece by folding the edge down ¼″ toward the wrong side, pressing, then folding again another ¾″. Stitch near the lower folded edge, leaving both sides open for inserting the elastic (figure 5).

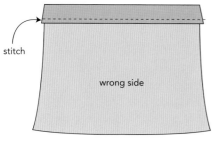

FIGURE 5

4 Use a large safety pin or a bodkin to help guide the elastic into the casing you just created (figure 6). Use your fingers to distribute the fabric evenly, and then stitch the side openings closed, making sure you catch the elastic on both sides.

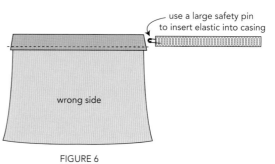

FIGURE 6

5 Place the back piece over the front piece right sides together (the front facing should now be at the bottom of the stack) and stitch/serge along both side edges using a ½″ seam allowance (figure 7). Turn the halter top right side out, press the side seams toward the back, and topstitch them down on the elastic.

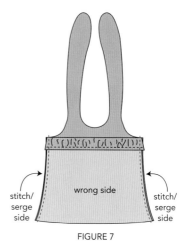

FIGURE 7

6 Create the hem band by placing one hem band piece over the other right sides together and stitching/serging along the short sides with a ½″ seam allowance (figure 8). Press the seams open if sewn or to one side if serged, and then fold the hem band in half wrong sides together, encasing the side seams as shown in figure 9. Press the folded edge.

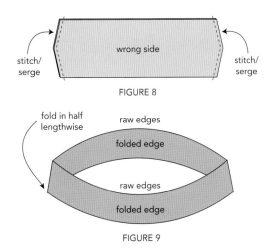

FIGURE 8

fold in half lengthwise

raw edges

folded edge

raw edges

folded edge

FIGURE 9

7 Attach the hem band to the bottom edge of the halter top by placing the raw edges together and stitching/serging all around with a ½" seam allowance (figure 10).

TIP: For a professional look, make sure both side seams are aligned on the hem band and top, and then pin in place to keep from shifting.

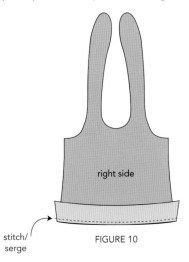

right side

stitch/
serge

FIGURE 10

8 When finished, press the hem band and seam allowance down, and then topstitch the seam down

using a stretch stitch or a coverstitch (see page 26 for different hemming techniques for knits). Sew a couple of decorative buttons just below the neckline and you're done (figure 11)!

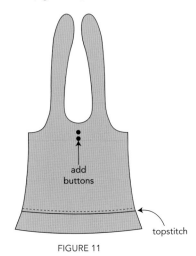

add buttons

topstitch

FIGURE 11

Our Tie Strap Halter looks super sweet paired up with our Twirly Tiered Skirt (page 64) and Leggings (page 75).

Mondrian shirt

NOTES ON FIT: Our Mondrian Shirt pattern was designed to hit about 2″ below the natural waist with a fairly loose fit around the torso. Always refer to the sizing chart provided when in doubt.

Inspired by the works of Dutch artist, Piet Mondrian (1872–1944), our *Mondrian Shirt* is a great example of color blocking and modern design. Known as "the father of geometric abstraction," Mondrian was a pivotal figure in the revolution of modern art that began with Cubism in the early twentieth century. Mondrian once stated that these strong vertical and horizontal lines were the "basic forms of beauty". I wholeheartedly agree and I think that this shirt design is striking in its modern simplicity, whether you make it out of all solid colors (like the artist himself would've done if he had designed clothing) or add in some cute prints for a whimsical touch. Pair it up with our Yoga Pants for a sporty look or with any of our skirt designs for a cute, comfy, and artsy look.

Child Sizing Chart			*Finished Mondrian Measurements*	
US Size	EURO Size	Child's Height	CHEST* CIRCUMFERENCE	SHIRT LENGTH*
2T	92	36.25″ (92 cm)	22″ W	15.75″ L
3T	98	38.75″ (98 cm)	23″ W	16.5″ L
4T	104	41″ (104 cm)	24″ W	17.25″ L
5T	110	43.5″ (110 cm)	25″ W	18″ L
6	116	45″ (116 cm)	26″ W	18.75″ L
7	122	48″ (122 cm)	27″ W	19.5″ L
8/9	128/134	50″-53″ (128-134 cm)	28″ W	20.25″ L
10	140	55″ (140 cm)	29″ W	21″ L

*CHEST is measured all around. *Shirt length assumes a 1/2″ hem.

SUPPLIES

You can use most stretch fabrics for your Mondrian Shirt including, but not limited to, cotton interlock, jerseys, double knits, rib knits, stretch velvet, or stretch velour, 58″/60″ wide. Refer to page 10 for more information on types of knits.

Use Pattern Pieces A (left-front piece), B (top-right piece), C (bottom-right piece), D (front bodice), E (back bodice), F (neck band), and G (sleeve/arm hole band) on page 6.

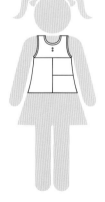

Sophie's Mondrian Shirt pairs up three solids and a strong stripe in coordinating colors to achieve a very linear and geometric look.

- ¾ yard all together OR about ½ yard to ⅓ yard of each of four different prints to achieve the color blocking effect (you can cut the smaller pieces out of scraps or remnants).

- **OPTIONAL:** Two decorative buttons, about ½" wide

- Coordinating thread

- Rotary cutter and self-healing mat, or dressmaking shears

- Flexible tape measure for determining your child's size

CUT

Cut the front bodice (Pattern Piece D) and back bodice (Pattern Piece E) on the fold as indicated on the pattern pieces. Cut 2 each of Pieces A, B, and C out of different fabric colors or patterns to achieve the "color block" look. Remember that you must cut the second set of Pieces A, B, and C on the reverse of the fabric, so fold the fabric in half first, as shown in our diagram, and then cut. Finally cut 2 sleeve (arm opening) bands and 1 neck band (figure 1). We use solid rib knit for the neck and sleeve bands in our sample shirts because it has great structure and recovery, plus it comes in a rainbow of colors and is readily available at most fabric stores.

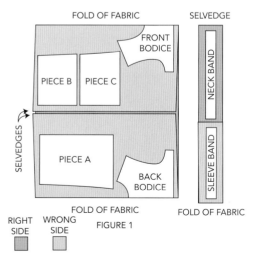

FOLD OF FABRIC   SELVEDGE

FRONT BODICE

PIECE B   PIECE C

NECK BAND

SELVEDGES

PIECE A

BACK BODICE

SLEEVE BAND

FOLD OF FABRIC   FOLD OF FABRIC

RIGHT SIDE   WRONG SIDE   FIGURE 1

ASSEMBLE

NOTE: It is very important to assemble the components of your Mondrian Shirt in the order given below. Label each piece so you know exactly where it goes and arrange them on your sewing table in the order they will be sewn together (figure 2). Think of it as piecing a quilt or constructing a puzzle.

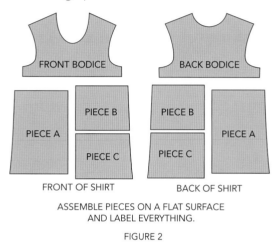

FRONT BODICE   BACK BODICE

PIECE B   PIECE B

PIECE A   PIECE A

PIECE C   PIECE C

FRONT OF SHIRT   BACK OF SHIRT

ASSEMBLE PIECES ON A FLAT SURFACE
AND LABEL EVERYTHING.

FIGURE 2

1 Start by assembling the full front and full back of the shirt, before stitching the shoulders and sides together. First, place Pieces B and C right sides together and stitch/serge across the horizontal seam using a ½" seam allowance (figure 3). Press the seam to one side.

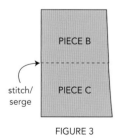

PIECE B

stitch/ serge

PIECE C

FIGURE 3

2   Next, place your assembled Pieces B and C over Piece A, right sides together, and stitch/serge the vertical center seam using a ½″ seam allowance (figure 4). Press this seam to one side.

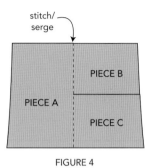

FIGURE 4

3   Next, place the full bottom piece over the front bodice right sides together, and stitch/serge across the horizontal bodice seam. Press this seam toward the bottom. Now you have the full front of the shirt (figure 5). Repeat steps 1–3 for the back of the shirt.

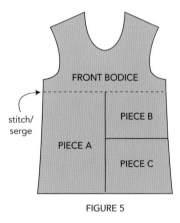

FIGURE 5

4   Once you have the full front and back of the shirt assembled, place them right sides together and pin the front bodice to the back bodice at the right shoulder. Stitch/serge using a ½″ seam allowance. *Don't join the other shoulder yet* (figure 6).

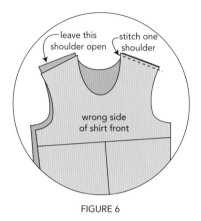

FIGURE 6

5   Fold the neck band (Pattern Piece F) in half lengthwise wrong sides together and press (figure 7). With the shirt right side out, pin the raw edges of the neck band to the neck opening, stretching the band slightly to fit. It helps to pin at the beginning and end, then stretch and pin in between, making sure the neck band is evenly stretched throughout (figure 8). Stitch/serge the raw edges together with a ½″ seam allowance. Press the neck band out, pressing the seam toward the garment. Topstitch ⅛″ from the seam using a stretch stitch.

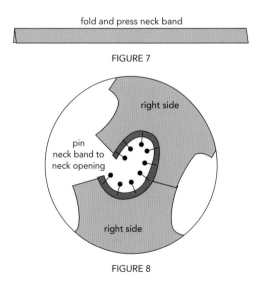

FIGURE 7

FIGURE 8

6 With right sides together, pin and then stitch/serge the other shoulder seam from the neck band to the arm opening (figure 9). Turn the garment right side out and machine bartack the neck band down at the seam.

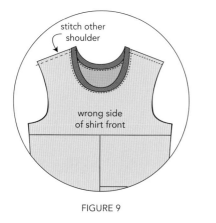

FIGURE 9

7 Fold the sleeve/arm hole band (Pattern Piece G) in half lengthwise wrong sides together and press. Stitch/serge the sleeve band to the edge of the arm opening (figure 10) in the same manner that you did with the neck band in step 5. Press outward, and then topstitch ⅛″ from the seam.

TIP: Try topstitching with a narrow zigzag stitch. It will give your shirt a funkier look while adding more elasticity to your seam.

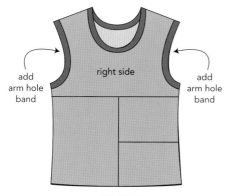

FIGURE 10

8 Turn the entire shirt inside out. With right sides together, pin the side seams of the garment together from the underarm to the bottom hem. Starting at the arm hole band, stitch/serge the sides of the shirt closed in one motion (figure 11).

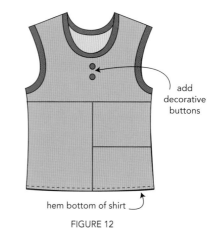

FIGURE 11

9 Turn your Mondrian Shirt right side out. Hand-stitch a couple of decorative buttons at the center front. Hem as desired (figure 12). See page 26 for hemming techniques with knits.

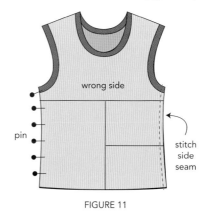

FIGURE 12

Maddie's Not-So-Plain Tee is made with a combination of patterned cotton interlocks, coordinating rib knit, and stretch lace trim at the hem.

not-so-plain tee

NOTES ON FIT: Our Not-So-Plain Tee pattern was designed to hit about 2″ below the natural waist. Always refer to the sizing chart provided when in doubt. If your girl has a long torso, cut the length on the tee's front and back bodice one or two sizes longer while keeping the width of the bodice to the correct size of the child. Likewise, if you want a shorter tee, cut your bodice one or two sizes shorter. Every child is unique, so don't be afraid to modify this pattern to fit her perfectly.

Everyone has that favorite T-shirt that fits just right—flattering, comfortable, and cute. I've tweaked this pattern so many times that I've lost count, changing the shape of the sleeves, shortening it a tad here and lengthening a bit there, then adding the right amount of binding to give it enough personality without too much bulk. Now that I've perfected this pattern, I'm ready to share it with you. I call it the *Not-So-Plain Tee* because with the right mixture of fabrics and trims, you can take it from basic to boutique in a snap.

Child Sizing Chart			*Finished T-Shirt Measurements*	
US Size	EURO Size	Child's Height	CHEST* CIRCUMFERENCE	T-SHIRT LENGTH*
2T	92	36.25″ (92 cm)	23″ W	15.75″ L
3T	98	38.75″ (98 cm)	24″ W	16.5″ L
4T	104	41″ (104 cm)	25″ W	17.25″ L
5T	110	43.5″ (110 cm)	26″ W	18″ L
6	116	45″ (116 cm)	27″ W	18.75″ L
7	122	48″ (122 cm)	28″ W	19.5″ L
8/9	128/134	50″-53″ (128-134 cm)	29″ W	20.25″ L
10	140	55″ (140 cm)	30″ W	21″ L

*CHEST is measured all around. *Shirt length assumes a 1/2″ hem.

SUPPLIES

You can use most stretch fabrics for your Not-So-Plain Tee including, but not limited to, cotton interlock, jerseys, double knits, rib knits, stretch velvet, or stretch velour, 58″/60″ wide. Refer to page 10 for more information on types of knits.

Use Pattern Pieces C (sleeve) and F (long-sleeve band) on page 7; and A (front), B (back), D (neck band), and E (short-sleeve band) on page 8.

- ½ yard of knit fabric for sizes 2T–6 OR ⅔ yard of knit fabric for sizes 7–10 (try experimenting with different prints!)

- If you desire contrast neck and sleeve bands as shown in our sample tees, you'll need ⅛ yard of rib knit or any solid knit with Lycra content.

- Coordinating thread
- Rotary cutter and self-healing mat, or dressmaking shears
- Flexible tape measure for determining your child's size
- **OPTIONAL:** stretch lace or other stretch trims to embellish hems.

CUT

Cut the front and back bodice on the fold as indicated on the pattern pieces. We love using two different fabric prints so it looks fun and funky from the side. This is a great way to accentuate a focal print on the front while using a solid, dot, or stripe for the supporting pieces (back panel and sleeves). Cut 2 sleeves, 2 sleeve bands, and 1 neck band (figure 1). We use solid rib knit for the neck and sleeve bands in our sample tees because it has great structure and recovery, plus it comes in a rainbow of colors and is readily available at most fabric stores.

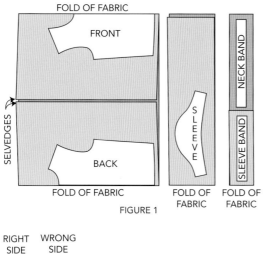

FIGURE 1

RIGHT SIDE WRONG SIDE

OPTIONAL: We love adding stretch trims to our hems for extra flair. If you want to do the same, cut your trims slightly longer than the bottom hem of your tee.

ASSEMBLE

1 Pin the front bodice to the back bodice at the right shoulder, right sides together. Stitch/serge using a ½" seam allowance. *Don't join the other shoulder yet* (figure 2).

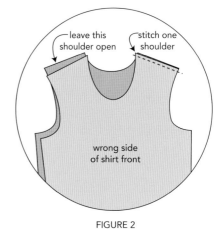

leave this shoulder open stitch one shoulder

wrong side of shirt front

FIGURE 2

2 Fold the neck band (Pattern Piece D) in half lengthwise wrong sides together and press (figure 3). With the bodice right side out, pin the raw edges of the neck band to the neck opening, stretching the band slightly to fit. It helps to pin at the beginning and end, and then stretch and pin in between, making sure the neck band is evenly stretched throughout (figure 4). Stitch/serge the raw edges together with a ½" seam allowance. Press the neck band out, pressing the seam toward the garment. Topstitch ⅛" from the seam using a stretch stitch.

fold and press neck band

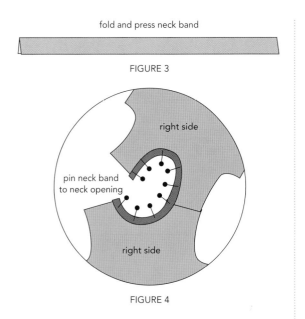

FIGURE 3

FIGURE 4

the sleeve (figure 6) in the same manner that you did with the neck band in step 2. Topstitch ⅛″ from the seam (figure 7).

TIP: Try topstitching with a narrow zigzag stitch. It will create a funkier look while adding more elasticity to your seam.

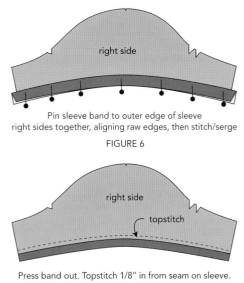

Pin sleeve band to outer edge of sleeve
right sides together, aligning raw edges, then stitch/serge

FIGURE 6

right side

topstitch

Press band out. Topstitch 1/8″ in from seam on sleeve.

FIGURE 7

3 With right sides together, pin and then stitch/serge the other shoulder seam from the neck band to the sleeve opening (figure 5). Turn the garment right side out and machine bartack the neck band down at the seam.

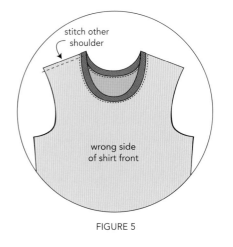

FIGURE 5

4 Fold the sleeve band (Pattern Piece E or F) in half lengthwise wrong sides together and press. Stitch/serge the sleeve band to the outer edge of

5 Attach the sleeves to the shirt, right sides together, aligning all notches (double notches on the back and single notches on the front). Press the sleeves outward and the seams toward the shirt bodice. Turn the entire shirt inside out. With right sides together, pin the underarm seams of the sleeves and side seams of the garment together, making sure your underarm seams are aligned. Starting at the bottom edge of the sleeve, stitch/serge the underarm and sides of the shirt closed in one motion (figure 8).

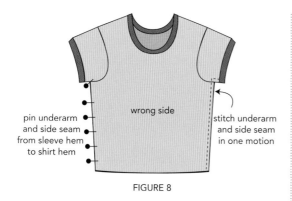

pin underarm
and side seam
from sleeve hem
to shirt hem

wrong side

stitch underarm
and side seam
in one motion

FIGURE 8

6 If you're adding a stretch trim to the hem, do this now before closing the other side (figure 9). Depending on the type of trim you are attaching, you can either stitch it to the raw edge of the fabric using a zigzag stitch, or sew it right sides together, turn it under, press, and topstitch it using a coverstitch or zigzag stitch, just like you did on the neck and sleeve bands.

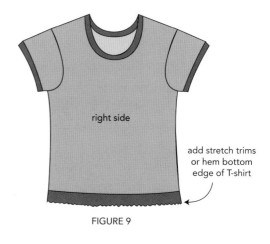

I love the look of these large stretch lace trims. They add color, texture, and style to any tee.

right side

add stretch trims
or hem bottom
edge of T-shirt

FIGURE 9

7 If you've chosen NOT to add trims to the hem, you can close up the other side of the tee and hem as desired. See page 26 for hemming techniques with knits.

Tween fashionistas, Maddie, Sophie, and Emersyn strike a pose in their Not-So-Plain Tees, Leg Warmers (page 46), and Fingerless Gloves (page 41).

Sophie loves her new V-neck sweater; it's cozy, soft, and warm and looks great with her favorite jeans.

contrast v-neck sweater

NOTES ON FIT: Our Contrast V-Neck Sweater pattern was designed to hit about 2″ below the natural waist. Always refer to the sizing chart provided when in doubt. If your girl has a long torso, cut the length on the sweater's front and back bodice one or two sizes longer while keeping the width of the bodice to the correct size of the child. Likewise, if you want a shorter sweater, cut your bodice one or two sizes shorter. Every child is unique, so don't be afraid to modify this pattern to fit her perfectly.

Oh the weather outside is frightful, but my Contrast V-Neck sweater is so delightful. **Perfect for layering over her favorite tee (how about our Not-So-Plain Tee?), this wardrobe staple is easy to pull-on and go and can be made light and airy for the fall or warm and cozy for the winter** depending on the fabrics you use. Complete the look with our Twirly Tiered Skirt, Leggings, and Stripwork Scarf for a handmade ensemble that delivers style and comfort. *And as long it warms me so, let it snow! Let it snow! Let it snow!*

Child Sizing Chart			Finished V-Neck Measurements	
US Size	EURO Size	Child's Height	CHEST* CIRCUMFERENCE	V-NECK SWEATER LENGTH*
2T	92	36.25″ (92 cm)	23″ W	15.75″ L
3T	98	38.75″ (98 cm)	24″ W	16.5″ L
4T	104	41″ (104 cm)	25″ W	17.25″ L
5T	110	43.5″ (110 cm)	26″ W	18″ L
6	116	45″ (116 cm)	27″ W	18.75″ L
7	122	48″ (122 cm)	28″ W	19.5″ L
8/9	128/134	50″-53″ (128-134 cm)	29″ W	20.25″ L
10	140	55″ (140 cm)	30″ W	21″ L

*CHEST is measured all around. *Sweater length assumes a 1/2″ hem.

SUPPLIES

Use soft and thick stretch fabrics for your Contrast V-Neck Sweater including, but not limited to, cotton interlock, double knits, rib knits, sweatshirt fleece, stretch terry, stretch velvet, or stretch velour, 58″/60″ wide. Refer to page 10 for more information on types of knits.

Use Pattern Pieces A (front facing), C (sleeve), E (bottom-front panel), F (long-sleeve band) and G (neck band) on page 7; and B (back piece) on page 8.

- 1 yard of knit fabric for sizes 2T–6 OR 1½ yards of knit fabrics for sizes 7–10 (try experimenting with different prints and fabric types!)

- If you desire contrast neck and sleeve bands as shown in our sample sweater, you'll need ⅛ yard of rib knit or any solid knit with Lycra content.

- Coordinating thread

- Rotary cutter and self-healing mat, or dressmaking shears

- Flexible tape measure for determining your child's size

CUT

Cut the bottom front panel, the back panel, and the neck band *on the fold* as indicated on the pattern pieces. Cut 2 front facings, 2 sleeves, and 2 sleeve bands as shown in figure 1. On our sample sweater, we used organic stretch velour for the back panel, sleeves, and front facing and added a patterned jersey as the accent fabric on the bottom front panel. We used solid rib knit for the neck and sleeve bands because it has great structure and recovery, plus it comes in a rainbow of colors and is readily available at most fabric stores.

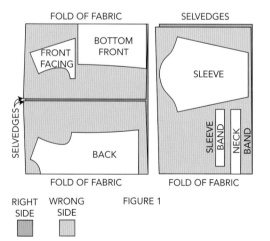

FIGURE 1

ASSEMBLE

1 Pin the front facings to the back panel at the shoulders, right sides together. Stitch/serge using a ½" seam allowance (figure 2).

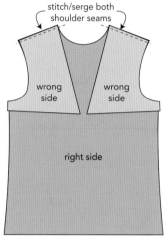

FIGURE 2

2 Fold the neck band (Pattern Piece G) in half lengthwise wrong sides together and press. With the bodice right side out, pin the raw edges of the neck band to the neck opening, stretching the band slightly to fit. It helps to pin at the beginning and end, and then stretch and pin in between, making sure the neck band is evenly stretched throughout (figure 3). Stitch/serge the raw edges together with a ½" seam allowance. Press the neck band out, pressing the seam toward the garment. Topstitch ⅛" from the seam on the garment side using a stretch stitch.

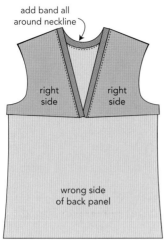

add band all around neckline

right side

right side

wrong side of back panel

FIGURE 3

3 Overlap the front facings slightly (no wider than the neck band) and baste together, creating the v-neck neckline, as shown in figure 4.

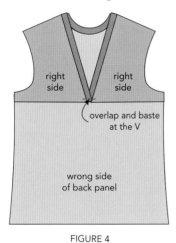

right side

right side

overlap and baste at the V

wrong side of back panel

FIGURE 4

4 With right sides together, stitch/serge the top edge of the bottom-front panel (Pattern Piece E) to the bottom edge of the front facings as shown in figure 5. Press the seam toward the bottom and topstitch on the bottom panel using a stretch stitch.

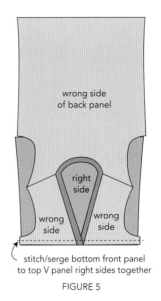

wrong side of back panel

right side

wrong side

wrong side

stitch/serge bottom front panel to top V panel right sides together

FIGURE 5

5 Fold the sleeve band (Pattern Piece F) in half lengthwise wrong sides together and press (figure 6). Stitch/serge the sleeve band to the outer edge of the sleeve, in the same manner that you did with the neck band in step 2. Topstitch ⅛″ from the seam (figure 7).

TIP: Try topstitching with a narrow zigzag stitch. It will create a funkier look while adding more elasticity to your seam.

fold and press sleeve band

FIGURE 6

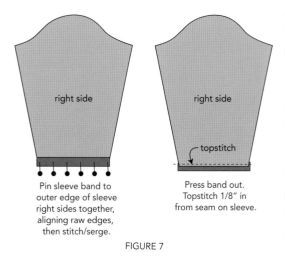

Pin sleeve band to outer edge of sleeve right sides together, aligning raw edges, then stitch/serge.

Press band out. Topstitch 1/8" in from seam on sleeve.

FIGURE 7

6 Attach the sleeves to the sweater, right sides together, aligning all notches (double notches on the back and single notches on the front) as shown in figure 8. Press the sleeves outward and the seams toward the shirt bodice.

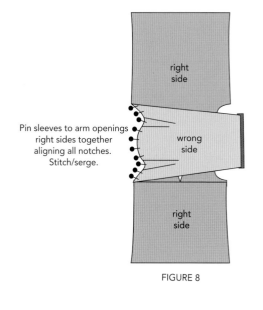

Pin sleeves to arm openings right sides together aligning all notches. Stitch/serge.

FIGURE 8

7 Turn the entire garment inside out. With right sides together, pin the underarm seams of the sleeves and side seams of the garment together, making sure your underarm seams are aligned. Starting at the bottom edge of the sleeve, stitch/serge the underarm and sides of the sweater closed in one motion (figure 9).

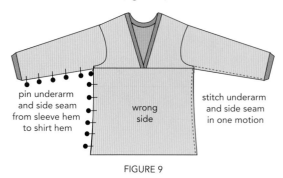

pin underarm and side seam from sleeve hem to shirt hem

stitch underarm and side seam in one motion

FIGURE 9

8 Hem your Contrast V-Neck Sweater as desired. See page 26 for hemming techniques with knits.

CHAPTER 5

dresses and ensembles

· · · ·

Anna is ready to party in h
Bubble Dress made with a
textured sweater knit for
the top and a denim knit f
the bottom. Her perfectly
matched Rosy Headband
and flower pin add extra
flair to her party ensemble.

Sydney looks oh, so
chic in her Bubble Dress made
with crushed velvet for the top and
a coordinating printed jersey for
the bottom. Her perfectly matched
Rosy Headband (page 32) and
rosette flower pins add extra flair
to her fun and funky ensemble.

bubble dress

NOTES ON FIT: Our Bubble Dress pattern was designed to hit right at the knee with a drop-waist design. This means the "bubble" part of the dress begins at the hip, not at the waist. Always refer to the sizing chart provided when in doubt: If you want a longer dress, cut the length on the front and back panels of the dress one or two sizes longer while keeping the width of the dress to the correct size of the child. Likewise, if you want a shorter dress, cut your panels one or two sizes shorter. Every child is unique, so don't be afraid to modify this pattern to fit her perfectly.

Our *Bubble Dress* is quite possibly the fanciest garment in this book. When I dreamt it up, I imagined it being worn at a wedding, a daddy-daughter dance, a school concert, or a holiday party. Use a thick fabric with a rich and luxurious texture, like a sweater knit or an organic velour, to give it a touch of glamour, or dress it down with cotton interlocks. The heavier the fabric, the poufier the skirt, so don't be afraid to pull out those stretch velvets, velours, and textured knits. For the warmer months, make a sleeveless version or add a cute little cap sleeve. Let's get this party started!

Child Sizing Chart			Finished Bubble Dress Measurements	
US Size	EURO Size	Child's Height	CHEST* CIRCUMFERENCE	BUBBLE DRESS LENGTH*
2T	92	36.25" (92 cm)	23" W	23" L
3T	98	38.75" (98 cm)	24" W	24" L
4T	104	41" (104 cm)	25" W	25" L
5T	110	43.5" (110 cm)	26" W	26" L
6	116	45" (116 cm)	27" W	27" L
7	122	48" (122 cm)	28" W	28" L
8/9	128/134	50"-53" (128-134 cm)	29" W	29" L
10	140	55" (140 cm)	30" W	31" L

*CHEST is measured all around. LENGTH assumes a 1/2" hem.

SUPPLIES

You can use most stretch fabrics for your Bubble Dress including, but not limited to, cotton interlock, jerseys, double knits, rib knits, stretch velvet, or stretch velour, 58″/60″ wide. Refer to page 10 for more information on types of knits.

Use Pattern Pieces D (inner skirt) on page 3; C (sleeve) on page 7; and A (front) and B (back) on page 8.

There are no pattern pieces for the outer skirt; use the chart on the following page to cut your panels.

- 1½ yards of knit fabric for sizes 2T–6 OR 2 yards for sizes 7–10
- Coordinating thread
- Rotary cutter, straightedge ruler, and self-healing mat; or dressmaking shears
- Flexible tape measure for determining your child's size

CUT

Cut the front and back panels on the fold as shown in figure 1. Cut 2 sleeves (either short or long) and 2 inner skirts as shown in figure 1. Cut 2 outer skirt panels using the chart below (maximum stretch of fabric running across the width). We used sweater knits and stretch velour for the top portion and cotton interlocks for the bubble skirts. Make sure you use a knit fabric with plenty of body for the skirt. Thin or slinky knits will not give it that "bubble" effect.

For the outer skirt:

Size 2T = 2 panels, 11″ high × 25½″ wide each

Size 3T = 2 panels, 11½″ high × 26″ wide each

Size 4T = 2 panels, 12″ high × 26½″ wide each

Size 5T = 2 panels, 12½″ high × 27″ wide each

Size 6 = 2 panels, 13″ high × 27½″ wide each

Size 7 = 2 panels, 13½″ high × 28″ wide each

Size 8/9 = 2 panels, 14″ high × 28½″ wide each

Size 10 = 2 panels, 14½″ high × 29″ wide each

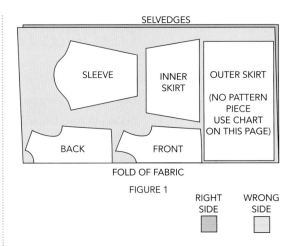

FIGURE 1

ASSEMBLE

1 Pin the front bodice to the back bodice at the shoulders, right sides together. Stitch/serge both shoulder seams using a ½″ seam allowance (figure 2).

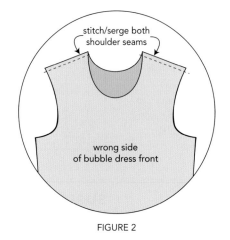

FIGURE 2

2 Hem the neck opening. Fold the neck edge in toward the wrong side ½″ and stitch close to the inner edge using a stretch stitch on your sewing machine or a coverstitch machine (figure 3).

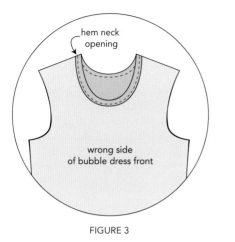

FIGURE 3

3 Hem the sleeves. Fold the sleeve's bottom edge in toward the wrong side ½″ and stitch close to the inner edge using a stretch stitch on your sewing machine or a coverstitch machine (figure 4).

wrong side of sleeve

hem sleeves

FIGURE 4

4 Attach the sleeves to the dress, right sides together, aligning all notches (double notches on the back and single notches on the front). Press the sleeves outward and the seams toward the dress (figure 5).

right side

wrong side

Pin sleeves to arm openings right sides together aligning all notches. Stitch/serge.

right side

FIGURE 5

5 Turn the entire top inside out. With right sides together, pin the underarm seams of the sleeves and side seams of the garment together, making sure your underarm seams are aligned. Starting at the bottom edge of the sleeve, stitch/serge the underarm and sides of the shirt closed in one motion (figure 6). Lay the top aside until you are ready to attach the bubble skirt to it.

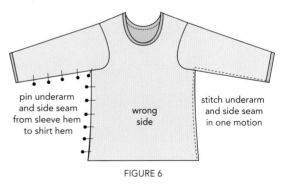

pin underarm and side seam from sleeve hem to shirt hem

wrong side

stitch underarm and side seam in one motion

FIGURE 6

6 With right sides together, pin and then stitch/serge along both side seams of your inner skirt using a ½″ seam allowance (figure 7). Turn right side out.

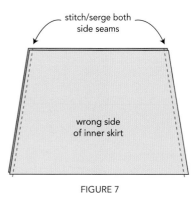

FIGURE 7

7 With right sides together, pin and then stitch/serge along both side seams of your outer skirt using a ½" seam allowance (figure 8). Turn right side out.

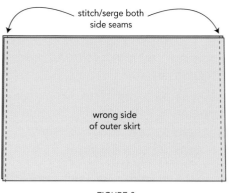

FIGURE 8

8 Gather the top and bottom edges of the outer skirt. Run a couple of long machine stitches along the top and bottom edges, and then gently pull the bobbin threads to gather the fabric. Use your fingers to evenly distribute the folds. Gather the top edge to the width of the inner skirt's top edge. Gather the bottom edge to the width of the inner skirt's bottom edge (figure 9).

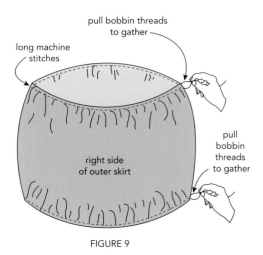

FIGURE 9

9 Turn the outer skirt inside out but leave the inner skirt right side out. Insert the inner skirt inside the outer skirt (figure 10).

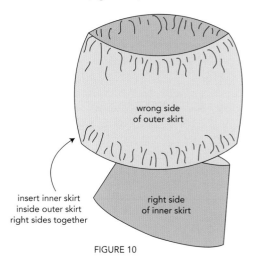

FIGURE 10

10 Quarter-mark the bottom edges of both skirts to ensure the gathers are evenly distributed and side seams are aligned. Pin and then stitch/serge them together with a ½" seam allowance (figure 11). *Don't sew the top edges yet.*

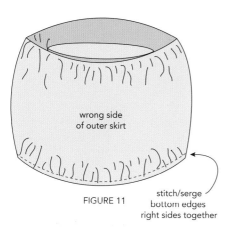

wrong side
of outer skirt

FIGURE 11

stitch/serge
bottom edges
right sides together

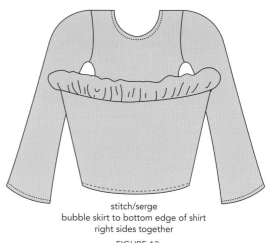

stitch/serge
bubble skirt to bottom edge of shirt
right sides together

FIGURE 13

11 Turn your entire skirt right side out (outer skirt on the outside) so the wrong sides are facing on your skirt. Align the side seams, and then quarter mark and pin the top edges together. Baste (figure 12).

13 Embellish your bubble dress with some cute rolled rosettes just like the ones we created for our Rosy Headband. See page 34 for full instructions. We added pin backs to the back of our rosettes so they could be easily removed and repositioned.

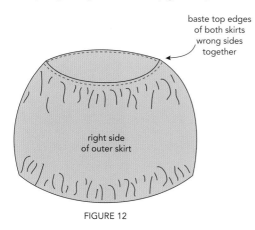

baste top edges
of both skirts
wrong sides
together

right side
of outer skirt

FIGURE 12

12 Insert your finished top inside the bubble skirt, right sides together. Align all side seams and pin in place. Stitch/serge the top edge of the bubble skirt to the bottom edge of the top with a ½″ seam allowance (figure 13).

Sydney is sporting a casual version of the Bubble Dress, made with short sleeves and using a playful polka dot cotton interlock from Michael Miller Fabrics.

Our Shirrley Tank Dress is the perfect layering piece for the cooler months. Just slip it over a long-sleeve tee and a pair of tights, and you're set to go!

shirrley tank dress

NOTES ON FIT: Our Shirrley Tank Dress pattern was designed to hit just below the knee. Always refer to the sizing chart provided when in doubt. If you prefer the dress to be a bit longer, cut the main dress panel one or two sizes longer while keeping the width of the panels to the correct size of the child. Likewise, if you want a shorter dress, cut your dress panel one or two sizes shorter. Every child is unique, so don't be afraid to modify this pattern to fit her perfectly!

I'm sure you've noticed the recent rise in popularity of the simple shirred dress as I have. They're showing up everywhere from department stores to upscale boutiques. Once you get the hang of this simple technique, you'll be shirring everything in sight—sleeves, dresses, waistbands, and bloomers. Kids love how soft and comfy they are, and you'll love that it conforms to all shapes so that a garment can technically "grow with her." So, let's get you started down that road to becoming a shirring maniac with the *Shirrley Tank Dress!*

Child Sizing Chart			*Cutting Guide for Shirrley Tank Dress*		
US Size	EURO Size	DRESS LENGTH*	DRESS PANEL CUT 1 PIECE	RUFFLED HEM	STRAPS CUT 2 PIECES**
2T	92	20"L	16"h x 30"w	1 Pc: 4"h x 58"w	8" long
3T	98	20.5"L	16.5"h x 32"w	1 Pc: 4"h x 58"w	9" long
4T	104	22"L	17"h x 34"w	1 Pc: 5"h x 58"w	10" long
5T	110	22.5"L	17.5"h x 36"w	1 Pc: 5"h x 58"w	11" long
6	116	24"L	18"h x 38"w	2 Pcs: 6"h x 40"w	12" long
7	122	25"L	19"h x 40"w	2 Pcs: 6"h x 42"w	12" long
8/9	128/134	26"L	20"h x 42"w	2 Pcs: 6"h x 44"w	13" long
10	140	27"L	21"h x 44"w	2 Pcs: 6"h x 46"w	13" long

*Dress length assumes a 1/2" hem. If finishing with a rolled hem, add 1/4" to the finished dress length
**Straps should be cut out of fold-over elastic, stretch lace, or equivalent.

SUPPLIES

You can use most stretch fabrics for your Shirrley Tank Dress including, but not limited to, cotton interlock, jerseys, rib knits, stretch velvet, or stretch velour, 58"/60" wide. Avoid thick fabrics with very little give, like double knits, because they will be more difficult to shirr. Refer to page 10 for more information on types of knits.

No pattern pieces are needed. Use the cutting guide provided on this page.

- For main dress panel: ½ yard of knit fabric for size 2T–6 OR ⅔ yard of knit fabric for sizes 7–10

fold over elastic (FOE) or ribbon or stretch lace

shirring

- For ruffled hem: ⅓ yard of coordinating knit fabric for all sizes
- 18″–24″ (depending on size of child) of ½″-wide knit elastic
- ½ yard of fold-over elastic, stretch lace, or equivalent stretch trims no more than ¾″ wide
- 1 spool of elastic thread
- Coordinating thread
- Rotary cutter and self-healing mat, or dressmaking shears
- Flexible tape measure for determining your child's size

CUT

Refer to the cutting guide provided on the previous page to determine what size to cut the main dress panel and ruffle panels. Remember that the maximum stretch of the fabric should always go side-to-side (along the longest of the measurements) on these panels. You should have one main dress panel, two ruffle panels, and two stretchy shoulder straps.

Cut a piece of ½″ knit elastic exactly 1″ shorter than the chest measurement of the child. If you don't have a child to measure, use the chart below for an approximate measure:

Sizes 2T and 3T = 18″ long

Sizes 4T and 5T = 20″ long

Sizes 6 and 7 = 22″ long

Sizes 8/9 and 10 = 24″ long

ASSEMBLE

1   Serge or finish the top edge of the dress panel with a zigzag stitch. Create an elastic casing at the top of your dress panel by folding the top edge down ¾″ toward the wrong side, pressing well, and then stitching over the serged/finished edge from one side of the dress to the other (figure 1) *Don't insert the elastic yet.* It's much easier to do this after you shirr the top portion of the dress.

NOTE: If you have a coverstitch machine, you don't need to serge or zigzag first; just stitch the raw edge down after pressing.

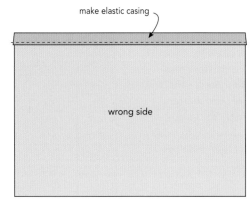

make elastic casing

wrong side

FIGURE 1

2   Determine how wide you want your shirred portion of the dress to be by measuring from the top folded edge down. Typically, you want the shirring to cover just the chest area to create an empire waist, so 4″–5″ is typical for the smallest sizes and no more than 7″ for the largest sizes. Mark the end of your shirred portion with a fabric-soluble marker, some masking tape, or a row of ballpoint pins (figure 2).

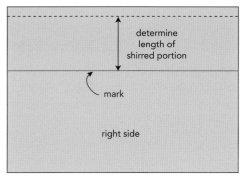

FIGURE 2

3 To shirr, you must wind your bobbin with elastic thread by hand, using a steady rhythm, not too tight and not too loose (figure 3)—practice makes perfect! Use regular thread for the top in a color that matches your fabric or is the least noticeable. Use your longest machine stitch and regular tension.

NOTE: If you've never shirred before, practice on a scrap of fabric first. Every machine is different, so play with your stitch length and tension until you get it just right. Sew at least three to four rows of shirring on your practice piece to get the feel of it. The piece should gather up nicely, and you should be able to stretch the fabric back to its original width without the threads snapping.

FIGURE 3

4 Place your fabric right side up on the machine. In other words, you want your elastic thread to be on the inside of your garment. Start your first row just below the elastic casing, no more than ¼″ down. Backstitch a couple of times at the beginning to secure the threads, and then straight-stitch all the way from one side of the dress panel to the other. When you reach the end, backstitch again to secure the threads, lift the needle and presser foot, turn the fabric all the way around, aligning the left edge of your presser foot with your first row of shirring (so you are now parallel to your first shirred row), and begin stitching again. Stitch your shirring rows exactly ¼″ apart. I use the edge of my presser foot as a guide so I know they're always evenly spaced. You won't see the fabric begin to pucker up until you've stitched three or more rows (figure 4).

FIGURE 4

5 When you've finished shirring, make sure to backstitch a couple of times to secure that elastic thread. Also, leave some long thread tails and tie them off by hand. Don't worry if you think the fabric did not gather as much as you expected it to. I'll show you a little trick I've learned along the way:

After (and only after) the entire top portion of your dress is shirred, remove the fabric from your machine and shoot it with a little bit of steam from your steam iron. Don't be afraid to get up close and personal; the steam won't hurt it, but you'll see the fabric gather up like magic right in front of your eyes (figure 5)!

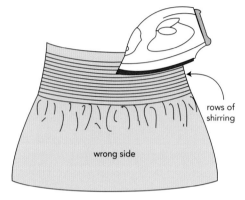

FIGURE 5

6   Once the top portion of your dress is fully shirred, go ahead and insert the ½″ knit elastic into the casing you created in step 1. Use a bodkin or large safety pin to help guide the elastic through, and secure both ends by stitching close to the edge of the casing (figure 6).

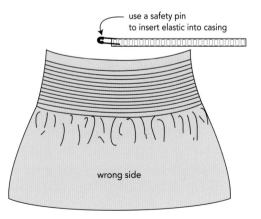

FIGURE 6

7   Now, you can close up the dress by folding it in half, right sides together, and stitching/serging from top to bottom along the open edges. Pinning is key to make sure all your shirring rows and your top and bottom edges are perfectly aligned (figure 7). Run another row of stitching across all the shirred rows within the seam allowance to reinforce this area. Finally, I like to press the seam to one side and topstitch it down to avoid extra bulk, especially where the elastic and elastic threads meet. Now your main dress is finished.

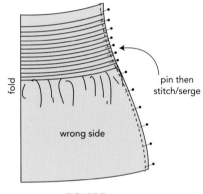

FIGURE 7

8   Create the ruffled hem by placing one ruffle piece over the other, right sides together, and stitching/serging across both short edges with a ½″ seam allowance to create a circular band (figure 8).

NOTE: If you're making sizes 2T–5, you only have one band to sew into a circle.

It's easier to hem this ruffle now, before gathering the top edge and attaching it to the dress. See page 26 for different hemming techniques for knit fabrics.

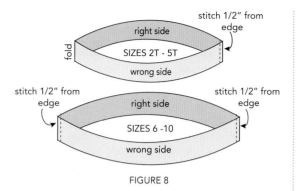

stitch 1/2" from edge

fold

right side

SIZES 2T - 5T

wrong side

stitch 1/2" from edge

stitch 1/2" from edge

right side

SIZES 6 -10

wrong side

FIGURE 8

9 Now it's time to gather the ruffle. Begin by running two lines of long gathering stitches along the top edge of the ruffle; the first row should be ⅛" from the top edge and the second row should be just ⅛" below the first. *Don't backstitch at the end.* You need those threads loose so you can grab and pull. Now using your fingers, grab the bobbin threads and carefully pull to gather the top edge of the ruffle to the same width as the dress panel (figure 9).

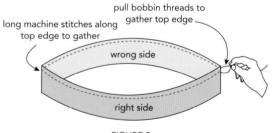

pull bobbin threads to gather top edge

long machine stitches along top edge to gather

wrong side

right side

FIGURE 9

10 Place the top portion of the dress on a flat surface so that the seam is perfectly centered on the back, and finger-press both sides of the dress to mark them (only on sizes 6–10). Place the ruffle over the dress panel right sides together so that the gathered edge of the ruffle is even with the bottom raw edge of the dress panel. Make sure the side seams on the ruffle are aligned with the

finger-pressed sides of the dress and place a pin on each side to prevent them from shifting.

NOTE: If making sizes 2T–5T, align the back seam of the ruffle with the back seam of the dress panel.

11 Pin all around, and then stitch/serge the raw edges together with a ½" seam allowance (figure 10). If you're serging, the blades of your serger will automatically trim off the gathering stitches, but if you're using a sewing machine, make sure you trim the seams down or remove the gathering stitches with a seam ripper. Press the ruffle and seam down when finished.

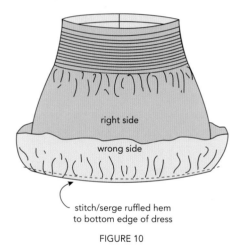

right side

wrong side

stitch/serge ruffled hem to bottom edge of dress

FIGURE 10

12 Try the dress on the child to determine where to attach the shoulder straps. Make sure the back seam of the dress is perfectly centered on her back and mark the positioning of the straps with a fabric-soluble marker. If the child is not around to measure, lay the dress flat on a table, mark the center front, then measure 1½" for sizes 2T–5T or 2" for sizes 6–10 from the center mark to the left and right. Do the same on the back of the dress. Mark both the front and the back of the dress, making sure you have 3" or 4" of space in between, depending on the size.

13 Fold the ends of your straps ½″ and stitch the shoulder straps at the front and back of the dress. You can either stitch them straight front to back or crisscross them at the back.

Giselle's dress was made using a solid color cotton interlock and a coordinating tonal floral for the ruffled hem band. We used fold-over elastic trimmed with a picot-edge elastic for the shoulder straps, and then we added little pink bows to make it that much cuter.

bloom dress

NOTES ON FIT: Our Bloom Dress pattern was designed to hit right at the knee. Always refer to the sizing chart provided when in doubt. If you want a longer dress, cut the length on the front and back panels of the dress one or two sizes longer while keeping the width of the dress to the correct size of the child. Likewise, if you want a shorter dress, cut your panels one or two sizes shorter. Every child is unique, so don't be afraid to modify this pattern to fit her perfectly.

Our *Bloom Dress* is a simple sheath-style dress with a slight A-line curve near the hem, which is as easy to sew as it is to wear. It just slips over the head like a comfy tee and has plenty of wiggle room for active kids. With the right choice of fabrics, this dress is versatile enough to be worn at casual and special occasions alike. Make it with long sleeves and pair it with our Leggings and Stripwork Scarf for the cooler months, or leave the sleeves off altogether for the perfect summer tank dress. It's so cute and comfortable, your little one's Bloom Dress will become a favorite in no time.

Child Sizing Chart			Finished Bloom Dress Measurements	
US Size	EURO Size	Child's Height	CHEST* CIRCUMFERENCE	BLOOM DRESS LENGTH*
2T	92	36.25" (92 cm)	23" W	21" L
3T	98	38.75" (98 cm)	24" W	23" L
4T	104	41" (104 cm)	25" W	24.5" L
5T	110	43.5" (110 cm)	26" W	26" L
6	116	45" (116 cm)	27" W	28" L
7	122	48" (122 cm)	28" W	29.5" L
8/9	128/134	50"-53" (128-134 cm)	29" W	31" L
10	140	55" (140cm)	30" W	33" L

*CHEST is measured all around. LENGTH assumes a 1/2" hem.

SUPPLIES

You can use most stretch fabrics for your Bloom Dress including, but not limited to, cotton interlock, jerseys, double knits, rib knits, stretch velvet, or stretch velour, 58"/60" wide. Refer to page 10 for more information on types of knits.

Use Pattern Pieces C (sleeve) and F (long-sleeve band) on page 7; and A (front), B (back), D (neck band), E (short-sleeve band) on page 8.

Use Template Pieces A (flower petals) and B (flower center) on page 3.

Anna and Sydney strut their stuff in their adorable Bloom Dresses made with designer cotton interlock knits.

- 1 yard of knit fabric for sizes 2T–6 OR 1¼ yards for sizes 7–10

- Small knit scraps or remnants of two contrasting fabric colors for the flower appliqué and bands

- Fusible web for adhering the appliqué to the dress

- Coordinating thread

- Rotary cutter, straightedge ruler, and self-healing mat; or dressmaking shears

- Flexible tape measure for determining your child's size

- **OPTIONAL:** stretch lace or other stretch trims to embellish hems

CUT

Cut the front and back panels on the fold as shown in figure 1. Cut 2 sleeves, 2 sleeve bands, and 1 neck band as shown in figure 1. We used cotton interlock for the neck and sleeve bands in our sample dresses, but you can also use solid rib knit for greater stretch and recovery. Cut 1 flower petal and 1 flower center out of contrasting fabric scraps using the templates provided.

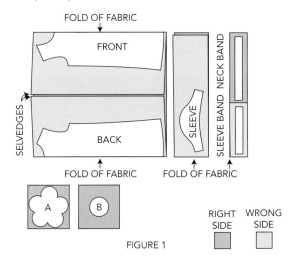

FIGURE 1

ASSEMBLE

1 Prepare the "Bloom" appliqué. Iron small strips of fusible web to the wrong side of your flower center appliqué, following manufacturer's instructions. Fuse the center to the petals, and then stitch them together using a zigzag stitch on your sewing machine (figure 2).

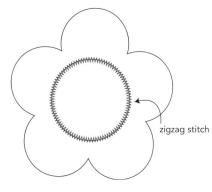

zigzag stitch

FIGURE 2

NOTES ON FUSIBLE WEB: I prefer to use a bonding agent, like fusible web, rather than pinning when appliquéing because it reduces the bulk and the pieces lay flatter when stitching. Fusible web is available by the yard in the interfacing section of fabric stores or in packaged quantities in the notions department. You can also find it in a small roll (like tape), which would be perfect for this project. Use the lightest weight possible for this project to minimize stiffness. Don't worry if it still feels a little stiff to you; just wash your garment when finished and it will soften up.

2 Using a straightedge ruler and a fabric marker, draw a line dividing the flower in half, and then cut it with a rotary cutter (figure 3). Iron small strips of fusible web to the wrong side of your flower appliqués.

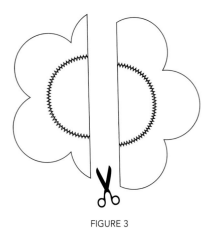

FIGURE 3

3   Placing your flower halves on the edges of the dress front panel as shown in figure 4, fuse and then stitch around the edges of the petals with a zigzag stitch. Baste across the side edges.

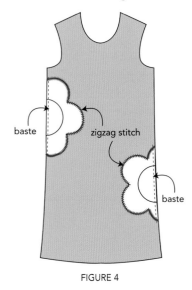

FIGURE 4

4   Pin the front bodice to the back bodice at the right shoulder, right sides together. Stitch/serge using a ½″ seam allowance. *Don't join the other shoulder yet* (figure 5).

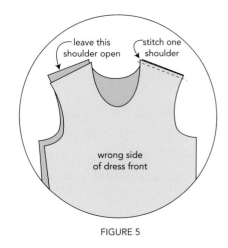

FIGURE 5

5   Fold the neck band (Pattern Piece D) in half lengthwise wrong sides together, and press (figure 6). With the dress right side out, pin the raw edges of the neck band to the neck opening, stretching the band slightly to fit. It helps to pin at the beginning and end, and then stretch and pin in between, making sure the neck band is evenly stretched throughout (figure 7). Stitch/serge the raw edges together with a ½″ seam allowance. Press the neck band out, pressing the seam toward the garment. Topstitch ⅛″ from the seam on the garment side, not on the band, using a stretch stitch.

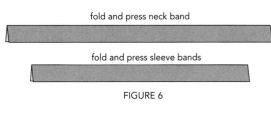

FIGURE 6

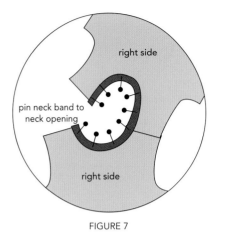

FIGURE 7

6 With right sides together, pin and then stitch/serge the other shoulder seam from the neck band to the sleeve opening (figure 8). Turn the garment right side out and machine bartack the neck band down at the seam.

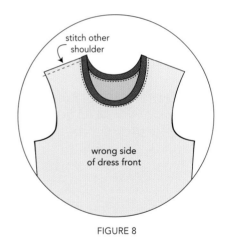

FIGURE 8

7 Fold the sleeve band (Pattern Piece E or F) in half lengthwise wrong sides together, and press. Stitch/serge the sleeve band to the bottom (straight) edge of the sleeve (Pattern Piece C) in the same manner that you did with the neck band

in step 5 (figure 9). Topstitch ⅛" from the seam (figure 10).

TIP: Try topstitching with a narrow zigzag stitch. It will create a funkier look while adding more elasticity to your seam.

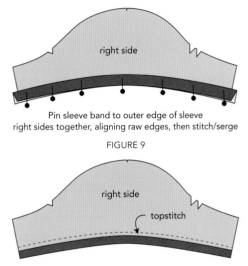

Pin sleeve band to outer edge of sleeve right sides together, aligning raw edges, then stitch/serge

FIGURE 9

Press band out. Topstitch 1/8" in from seam on sleeve.

FIGURE 10

8 Attach the sleeves to the dress, right sides together, aligning all notches (double notches on the back and single notches on the front). Press the sleeves outward and the seams toward the dress.

9 Turn the entire dress inside out. With right sides together, pin the underarm seams of the sleeves and side seams of the garment together, making sure your underarm seams are aligned. Starting at the bottom edge of the sleeve, stitch/serge the underarm and sides of the shirt closed in one motion (figure 11).

Pair your Bloom Dress up with some funky tights, boots, and a light cardi for the cooler months.

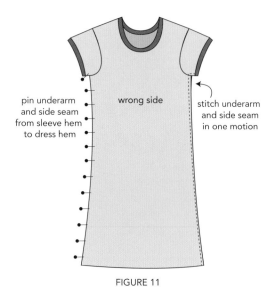

pin underarm
and side seam
from sleeve hem
to dress hem

wrong side

stitch underarm
and side seam
in one motion

FIGURE 11

10 If you're adding a stretch trim to the hem, do this now before closing the other side. Depending on the type of trim you are attaching, you can either stitch it to the raw edge of the fabric using a zigzag stitch, or sew it right sides together, turn it under, press and topstitch it using a coverstitch or zigzag stitch.

11 If you've chosen not to add trims to the hem, you can close up the other side of the dress and hem as desired. See page 26 for hemming techniques with knits.

The Bloom Dress
is cute enough
for a party and
comfortable
enough for play.

A family trip to the beach is that much more fun with custom-made swimsuits in their favorite colors and prints.

swimsuit

NOTES ON FIT: Our Swimsuit pattern was designed to have a very snug fit like most swimsuits do. Always refer to the sizing chart provided when in doubt. If you want a looser fit, you can cut the tankini panels one or two sizes wider. Likewise, you can go down in size (width) if you want a tighter fit. Every child is unique, so don't be afraid to modify this pattern to fit her perfectly.

Splish, splash! She'll sure be a smash at her next beach bash. This two-piece *Swimsuit* features a tankini-style top and a skort-style bottom—so cute and perfect for easy trips to the potty. Because we bind it with fold-over elastic, you can sew it in a flash, without spending a lot of cash. No doubt it'll be her favorite in her swimsuit stash!

	Child Sizing Chart			*Finished Swimsuit Measurements*		
US Size	EURO Size	Child's Height	CHEST* CIRCUMF.	TANKINI LENGTH*	SKORT LENGTH*
2T	92	36.25" (92 cm)	17" W	8" L	8" L
3T	98	38.75" (98 cm)	18" W	9" L	8.5" L
4T	104	41" (104 cm)	19" W	10" L	9" L
5T	110	43.5" (110 cm)	20" W	11" L	9.5" L
6	116	45" (116 cm)	21" W	12" L	10" L
7	122	48" (122 cm)	22" W	13" L	10.5" L
8/9	128/134	50"-53" (128-134 cm)	23" W	14" L	11" L
10	140	55" (140 cm)	24" W	15" L	12" L

*CHEST is measured all around. LENGTH assumes a 1/2" hem.

SUPPLIES

I recommend using only swim-wear or active-wear fabrics, like a Nylon-Lycra (spandex) blend with a four-way stretch. Refer to page 10 for more information on types of knits.

Use Pattern Pieces A (front) and B (back) on page 9 for the tankini portion of the swimsuit.

Use Pattern Pieces C (skort front and back), D (skirt panel), and E (waistband) on page 9 for the skort portion of the swimsuit.

- 1 yard of swimsuit fabric for sizes 2T and 3T, 1¼ yards for sizes 4T–6, OR 1½ yards for sizes 7–10
- 1 yard of fold-over elastic for sizes 2T and 3T OR 2 yards of fold-over elastic for sizes 4T–10 for tankini straps
- Coordinating thread

FRONT   BACK

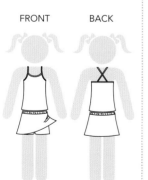

- Rotary cutter, straightedge ruler, and self-healing mat; or dressmaking shears
- Flexible tape measure for determining your child's size

CUT

Cut the front and back tankini panels on the fold as shown in figure 1. Then cut 2 short pieces, 2 skirt pieces, and 2 waistband pieces as shown in figure 1 for the skort portion of the swimsuit.

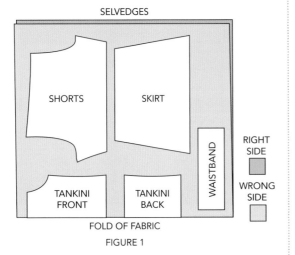

FIGURE 1

Cut 1 short and 1 long piece of fold-over elastic (FOE), according to the chart below, for the tankini binding:

Size 2T: one short piece at 4½" long and one long piece at 29" long

Size 3T: one short piece at 5" long and one long piece at 31" long

Size 4T: one short piece at 5½" long and one long piece at 33" long

Size 5T: one short piece at 6" long and one long piece at 35" long

Size 6: one short piece at 6½" long and one long piece at 37" long

Size 7: one short piece at 7" long and one long piece at 39" long

Size 8/9: one short piece at 7½" long and one long piece at 42" long

Size 10: one short piece at 8" long and one long piece at 44" long

ASSEMBLE THE TANKINI

1   Add the *short piece* of fold-over elastic (FOE) to the top edge of the tankini front panel as shown in figure 2. Wrap the FOE around the raw edge of the fabric using the groove down the middle of the FOE to fold it in half, and then pin it in place, stretching the FOE ever so slightly but not stretching the fabric at all. If you don't stretch the FOE slightly, it will result in a wavy edge, but if you stretch it too much, it will gather the edge. Practice on a small scrap of fabric until you get the right amount of stretch. Use a zigzag stitch on your sewing machine to stitch the FOE on, backstitching at the ends to reinforce it. Trim any excess off. See page 16 for additional information about FOE.

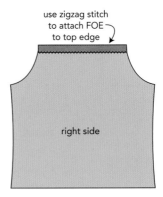

FIGURE 2

2 Place the front and back tankini panels right sides together, and then stitch/serge along both side edges with a ½″ seam allowance (figure 3).

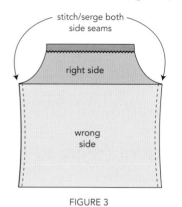

stitch/serge both side seams

right side

wrong side

FIGURE 3

3 Turn the tankini right side out. Finger-press the center mark of the back panel, and finger-press the center of the long piece of FOE. Aligning finger-pressed marks, pin the center of the FOE to the center back, and then begin folding and pinning the FOE to the edge of the tankini, working your way up one side until you reach the top front of the tankini. Then just fold and pin the remainder of the FOE to itself, creating the shoulder strap (figure 4). Do the same thing on the other side, starting at the center back and ending at the strap.

NOTE: Before you begin stitching, measure the length of the two shoulder straps to make sure they are equal. If one strap is shorter than the other, unpin it and re-pin it, stretching it ever so slightly, until they are equal.

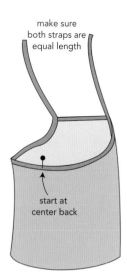

make sure both straps are equal length

start at center back

FIGURE 4

4 Using a zigzag stitch and beginning at the raw end of one shoulder strap, stitch the FOE in place, covering the edge of the tankini. When the FOE straps meet the top front FOE, backstitch and forward stitch a couple of times to reinforce these areas. End your zigzag stitch at the other end of the strap.

NOTE: If your child is around, this is the best time to try on the tankini top to make sure the straps are the right length. If they are too long after you crisscross them in the back, trim off the excess.

5 Measure an equal distance from the center back, mark, pin the straps on the inside of the FOE border, and then stitch them in place with a zigzag stitch (figure 5). Stitch several times over your first stitches to reinforce this area.

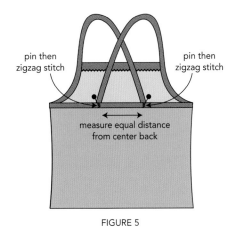

pin then zigzag stitch

pin then zigzag stitch

measure equal distance from center back

FIGURE 5

6 Hem your tankini, and it's done!

ASSEMBLE THE SKORT

7 Go ahead and hem both shorts legs while they are flat, since the opening will be too narrow to hem after they are sewn together, especially on the smaller sizes. To hem, fold up a ½" hem allowance,

press the edge, and then stitch as shown in figure 6. If you own a coverstitch machine, you can get a very professional finish, but a stretch twin needle on your sewing machine can achieve a similar look. Of course, you can always just use a stretch stitch or a zigzag stitch on your sewing machine (see page 26 for hemming techniques for knit fabrics).

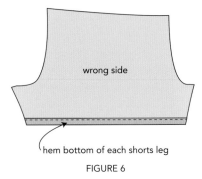

wrong side

hem bottom of each shorts leg

FIGURE 6

8 Place one shorts piece over the other right sides together, aligning all sides and notches, and then pin. Using a ½" seam allowance, stitch/serge the front and back center seams as shown in figure 7. If you're not serging the edge, trim the seam allowances down to ¼" to reduce bulk.

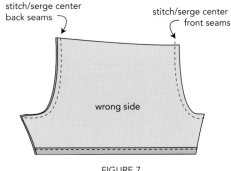

stitch/serge center back seams

stitch/serge center front seams

wrong side

FIGURE 7

9 Now, open up your shorts and align the inside leg seams right sides together, matching the notches and crotch seams. Pin and then stitch/serge the inseam from one side to the other using a ½″ seam allowance (figure 8). Again, if you're not serging the edge, trim the seam allowances down to ¼″ to reduce bulk. Lay the shorts aside until you are ready to attach them to the skirt and waistband.

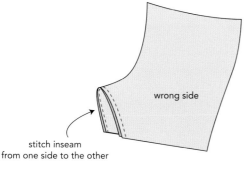

stitch inseam
from one side to the other

FIGURE 8

10 Sew the side seams on the skirt pieces right sides together with a ½″ seam allowance (figure 9). Hem the bottom edge of the skirt using your preferred method.

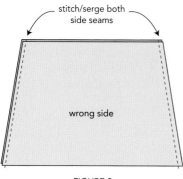

stitch/serge both
side seams

wrong side

FIGURE 9

11 Finger-press the front and back centers of the skirt. With both pieces right sides out, insert the shorts inside the skirt, aligning the center seam of the shorts with the finger-pressed marks on the skirt. Pin and baste at the top edges to prevent it from shifting (figure 10).

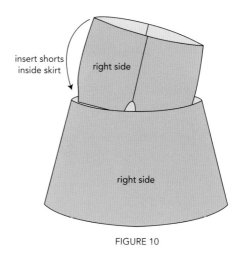

insert shorts
inside skirt

right side

right side

FIGURE 10

12 Place the two waistband pieces right sides together and stitch both short side seams with a ½″ seam allowance, creating a fabric circle (figure 11).

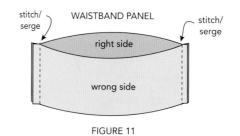

stitch/
serge

WAISTBAND PANEL

stitch/
serge

right side

wrong side

FIGURE 11

13 Fold the waistband piece in half lengthwise wrong sides together, and press the top folded edge (figure 12).

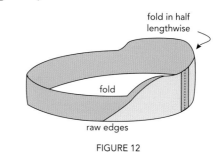

fold in half
lengthwise

fold

raw edges

FIGURE 12

14 Place the waistband panel over the skort right sides together, aligning the side seams. Stitch/serge the waistband to the skort, stretching the raw edges of the waistband slightly to fit (figure 13). The no-elastic waistband is naturally narrower than the skort because it needs to fit snugly on the child to hold up the skort.

NOTE: If you are using a serger, the blades of the serger will automatically trim off the basting stitches. If you are using a sewing machine, make sure you use a stretch stitch and remove the basting stitches afterward.

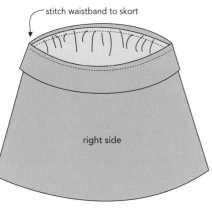

stitch waistband to skort

right side

FIGURE 13

Sophie's Mod swimsuit is made with a Marimekko lycra and trimmed in blue FOE.

Sydney loves her new rainbow swimsuit and is thrilled that it doubles as a cool summertime outfit!

Sydney is oh, so fashionable at the beach with her pink cover-up.

swim cover-up

NOTES ON FIT: Our Swim Cover-up pattern was designed to hit just above the knee. Always refer to the sizing chart provided when in doubt. If you want a longer or shorter cover-up, adjust the length of the front and back panels accordingly while keeping the width intact. Every child is unique, so don't be afraid to modify this pattern to fit her perfectly.

Every girl needs something cute to toss over her swimsuit after a dip in the pool or during a family trip to the beach. Our *Swim Cover-up* comes with extra special details that add not only style but also functionality. The hood may look super sweet but also helps absorb extra moisture from her wet hair. The kangaroo pocket keeps little hands warm and is also perfect to store swim goggles when not in use. And of course, the ruffled hem band adds an extra touch of flair so your little fashionista can feel like the belle of the ball at her next pool party.

Child Sizing Chart			Finished Cover-up Measurements	
US Size	EURO Size	Child's Height	CHEST* CIRCUMFERENCE	SWIM COVER-UP LENGTH*
2T	92	36.25" (92 cm)	23" W	20" L
3T	98	38.75" (98 cm)	24" W	22" L
4T	104	41" (104 cm)	25" W	23.5" L
5T	110	43.5" (110 cm)	26" W	25" L
6	116	45" (116 cm)	27" W	27" L
7	122	48" (122 cm)	28" W	28.5" L
8/9	128/134	50"-53" (128-134 cm)	29" W	30" L
10	140	55" (140 cm)	30" W	32" L

*CHEST is measured all around. LENGTH includes a 3" ruffled band and a 1/2" hem.

SUPPLIES

You can use most stretch fabrics for this pattern, but I recommend using thicker, more absorbent fabrics like stretch terry, stretch fleece, or stretch velour, 58"/60" wide, if you are using it as a Swim Cover-up. Of course, you can make this pattern as a cute hooded dress, in which case you can use pretty much any stretch fabric you desire. Refer to page 10 for more information on types of knits.

Use Pattern Pieces C (sleeve), D (hood), and E (kangaroo pocket) on page 7; A (front) and B (back) on page 8. There is no pattern piece for the ruffled hem band.

- 1 yard of knit fabric for sizes 2T and 3T, 1¼ yards for sizes 4T–6, OR 1½ yards for sizes 7–10

FRONT   BACK

- 1½ yards of fold-over elastic for sizes 2T–5T OR 2 yards for sizes 6–10, for hood and sleeve bands

NOTE: If you don't have fold-over elastic, you can make this pattern without it by stitching a narrow hem on your sleeves and hood or adding a thin self-binding.

- Coordinating thread
- Rotary cutter, straightedge ruler, and self-healing mat; or dressmaking shears
- Flexible tape measure for determining your child's size

CUT

Cut the front and back panels on the fold as shown in figure 1. Don't forget that to accommodate for the added height of the ruffled hem band, you need to trim 4″ off the bottom edge on the front and back dress panels. Fold the fabric in half right sides together so the selvedges meet on one side, and then cut 2 sleeves, 2 hoods, and 2 kangaroo pockets as shown in figure 1. To make the ruffled band, cut a 4″ strip on the fold that spans the full width of the fabric as shown in figure 1. The maximum stretch of the fabric should go widthwise across the ruffle band.

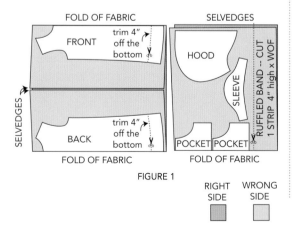

FIGURE 1

RIGHT SIDE   WRONG SIDE

ASSEMBLE

1 Assemble the hood by pinning the two sides right sides together and stitching/serging around the rounded edge as shown in figure 2.

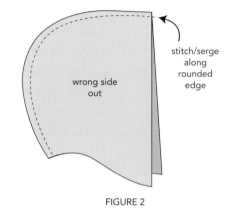

FIGURE 2

2 Turn the hood right side out and attach the fold-over elastic (FOE) to the outer/front edge of the hood as shown in figure 3. See page 16 for additional information about FOE. No need to trim the FOE to size; just wrap it around the raw edge of the hood using the groove down the middle of the FOE to fold it in half, and then pin it in place, stretching the FOE ever so slightly but not stretching the fabric at all. This will gather the front edge of the hood slightly. Use a zigzag stitch on your sewing machine to stitch the FOE to the hood, backstitching at the beginning and end to reinforce it. Trim the excess FOE off.

NOTE: If you don't have FOE to use, you can just stitch a narrow hem on the front edge of the hood as shown in figure 3.

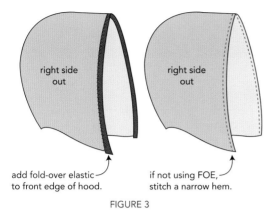

add fold-over elastic to front edge of hood.

if not using FOE, stitch a narrow hem.

FIGURE 3

3 Attach the FOE to the outer edge of each sleeve just like you did in step 2 for the hood (figure 4). You can see in the photo how we attach the FOE to the edge of the sleeve with a zigzag stitch. Stitch a narrow hem if you're not using FOE.

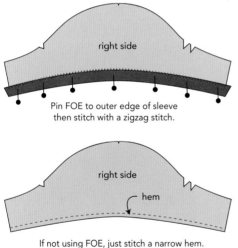

right side

Pin FOE to outer edge of sleeve then stitch with a zigzag stitch.

right side

hem

If not using FOE, just stitch a narrow hem.

FIGURE 4

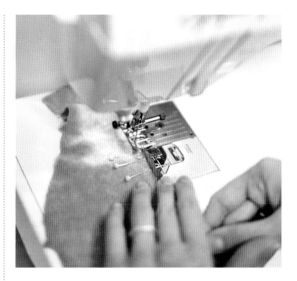

4 Place your kangaroo pocket pieces right sides together and pin. Stitch around the full perimeter of the pocket with a ½″ seam allowance, leaving a small gap at the bottom for turning the pocket (figure 5). Trim all corners and clip the inner curves to reduce bulk, and then turn the pocket right side out.

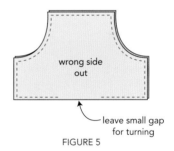

wrong side out

leave small gap for turning

FIGURE 5

5 Use a blunt tool, like a bamboo creaser or a wooden chopstick, to ensure all corners are square. Press well, and then topstitch on the curved edges *only*, as shown in figure 6.

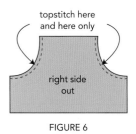

topstitch here
and here only

right side
out

FIGURE 6

6 Place the pocket on the front panel of the Swim Cover-up exactly 4½" from the bottom edge. Pin the pocket in place, making sure it is centered left to right, and then stitch all the straight edges down, as shown in figure 7, making sure to reinforce all the corners. Leave both curved edges unstitched to create the pocket openings.

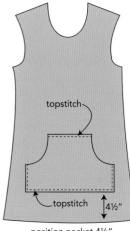

topstitch

topstitch

4½"

position pocket 4½"
from bottom edge of front panel
then topstitch where indicated

FIGURE 7

7 Pin the front bodice to the back bodice at the shoulders, right sides together. Stitch/serge both shoulder seams using a ½" seam allowance (figure 8).

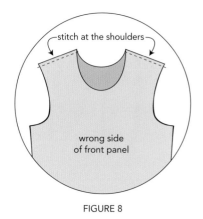

stitch at the shoulders

wrong side
of front panel

FIGURE 8

8 Attach the sleeves to the dress, right sides together, aligning all notches (double notches on the back and single notches on the front). Press the sleeves outward and the seams toward the bodice.

9 Turn the entire garment inside out. With right sides together, pin the underarm seams of the sleeves and the side seams of the garment together, making sure your underarm seams are aligned. Starting at the bottom edge of the sleeve, stitch/serge the underarm and sides of the garment closed in one motion (figure 9).

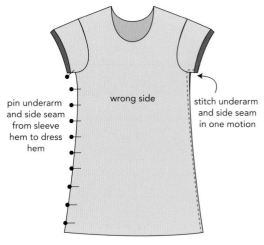

pin underarm
and side seam
from sleeve
hem to dress
hem

wrong side

stitch underarm
and side seam
in one motion

FIGURE 9

The kangaroo pocket on our Swimsuit Cover-up is perfect to store goggles, swim caps, or small beach toys.

10 Attach the hood. Turn the dress right side out, fold the back dress panel in half, and finger-press the center mark right at the neck opening. With right sides together, align the center seam of the hood with the finger-pressed center mark on the back of the dress. Pin in place. Without stretching the fabric at all, pin the raw edges of the hood, starting at the center back, all along the perimeter of the neck opening, ending a little past the center front. The front edges of the hood should overlap no more than 1″ along the center front of the dress. Stitch/serge (figure 10).

NOTE: It's very important that this seam has plenty of elasticity so the child can easily pull the garment over her head without the threads snapping, so if you're not using a serger, make sure you stitch the hood using a stretch stitch, like a three-step zigzag or a stem stitch, on your sewing machine. See "Sewing Knits with Your Sewing Machine" on page 24, for more information on stretch stitches.

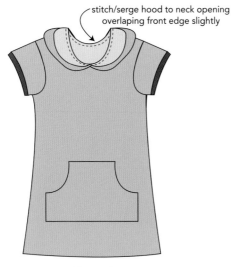

stitch/serge hood to neck opening overlaping front edge slightly

FIGURE 10

11 Create the ruffled hem band. Stitch/serge the hem band along the short edges, right sides together, creating a circular band (figure 11).

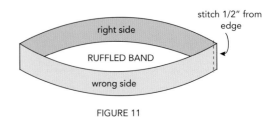

right side

RUFFLED BAND

wrong side

stitch 1/2″ from edge

FIGURE 11

12 Gather the hem band. Begin by running two lines of long gathering stitches along the top edge of the band; the first row should be ⅛″ from the top edge and the second row should be just ⅛″ below the first. *Don't backstitch at the end.* You need those threads loose so you can grab and pull them. Now using your fingers, grab the bobbin threads and carefully pull to gather the top edge of the band to the same width as the bottom edge of the garment (figure 12).

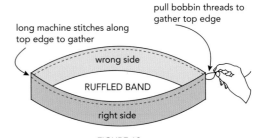

long machine stitches along top edge to gather

pull bobbin threads to gather top edge

wrong side

RUFFLED BAND

right side

FIGURE 12

Anna's cover-up is made with stretch French terry in a crisp white with lime green and lemon yellow fold-over elastic binding. Sydney's pink-on-pink cover-up is made with organic velour.

13 Attach the band to the dress by placing them right sides together so that the gathered edge of the band is even with the bottom raw edge of the dress. Make sure the seam on the band is aligned with the center back of the dress. Pin all around, and then stitch/serge the edges together with a ½" seam allowance (figure 13). If you're serging, the blades of your serger will automatically trim off the gathering stitches, but if you're using a sewing machine, make sure you trim the seams down or remove the gathering stitches with a seam ripper.

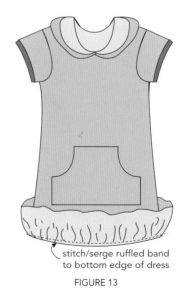

stitch/serge ruffled band
to bottom edge of dress

FIGURE 13

14 Hem the ruffled band as desired. See page 26 for information on different hemming techniques.

Glossary

Backstitch: To sew in reverse for a few stitches in order to add strength to a seam and prevent it from unraveling.

Ballpoint needle: A sewing machine needle with a rounded tip that allows it to pass through fabric without cutting the yarns of the fabric. Its most frequent application is its use in the sewing of knit fabrics.

Bartack: A tight row of stitches, parallel to the seam, that reinforces and helps keep the seam allowance flat against the body.

Baste: To temporarily sew with long removable stitches in order to keep two layers of fabric from shifting.

Bodkin: A blunt large-eyed needle used for drawing elastic or ribbon through a casing.

Casing: A narrow passage for elastic, ribbon, or cord as in the waistband of a garment, made by folding over a small strip of fabric at its edge along its width and sewing it in place.

Crosswise: The crosswise grain is made up of threads that run perpendicular to the selvedge edges.

Drape: The way in which a fabric falls or hangs.

Elasticity: The state or quality of being elastic or stretchy.

Facing: The area of a garment or sewn item that turns to the inside, giving a finished appearance to what would otherwise just be a raw edge of fabric.

Finger-press: Creating a crease or mark on the fabric by folding it and applying pressure with your fingers.

Gathers: A series of small tucks of fabric, controlled and held in place by stitches and providing visible fullness.

Gores: Vertical division within a garment, usually tapered panels, narrower at the upper edge than the lower edge, seamed together to add fullness to a garment—may be functional or decorative.

Grainline: A line drawn on a sewing pattern to indicate the direction of pattern placement on the fabric. Align this mark on the pattern pieces with the vertical grain of the fabric, which runs parallel to the selvedge.

Nap: A raised texture in the fabric that requires all parts of the garment to be cut in the same direction. Velvet and velour are fabrics with nap.

Notch: Small cuts or wedges made within the seam of a garment piece to aid in correct assembly.

Notion: All the materials, other than the fabric and pattern, required to produce a garment.

Pivot: Leaving the sewing machine needle in the fabric, raise the presser foot, turn the fabric at a sharp angle, lower the presser foot, and continue stitching.

Quarter-mark: In sewing, it refers to dividing the length of a piece into four equal parts and marking the fabric at each quarter to ease in garment construction, especially when joining two rounded pieces of different lengths.

Recovery: The tendency of a fabric or notion to return to its original shape after it has been stretched.

Rib/Rib knit: A fabric knitted with a visible ribbed texture on both sides, perfect to use for neck and sleeve bands due to their great elasticity and recovery factors.

Seam allowance: The amount of fabric between the cut edge of your piece and the stitched line (or seam).

Selvedge: Edge of the fabric that is woven/finished to prevent raveling. Selvedges run parallel to the vertical grain of the fabric.

Raw edge: Any unfinished cut edge of fabric.

Rotary cutter: A cutting tool with a round blade that is capable of slicing through one or more layers of fabric. Resembling a pizza cutter, rotary cutters are available with several different sizes of cutting discs and handle types.

Ruffle: Decorative, gathered, or pleated strips of fabric or ribbon sewn to the garment.

Serge: To overcast the raw edges of a fabric in order to prevent unraveling.

Shirring: Parallel rows of stretchy gathers made in the body of the garment using elastic thread.

Shrinkage: The act of a fabric shrinking in the process of washing. Knit fabrics usually shrink more along the lengthwise grain than along the crosswise grain.

Stitch in the Ditch: Stitching directly on top of a finished seam line to create a quilted effect. The stitch goes through all layers and becomes almost invisible.

Synthetic: A man-made fiber created through a chemical process, such as nylon, polyester, or acrylic as opposed to those of natural origin, such as cotton, wool, or silk.

Topstitch: Also called *Edgestitch*, a line of stitching that runs parallel to the seam or fold and is used to give a more finished look to your piece by helping the seam lie flat. Use a medium machine stitch length and stitch 1/8″ from edge/seam.

Resources

www.modkidboutique.com

My website. From my home page you can click over to my blog, my Flickr groups, my Twitter feed, my Facebook Fan Page and my YouTube channel (yes, I love social media!). Also, you can view all of my existing fabric collections and sewing patterns plus browse a comprehensive list of domestic and international retailers that carry all of my products.

www.michaelmillerfabrics.com

My fabric family. A manufacturer of wonderful modern and retro-inspired fabrics headquartered in New York. Search for fabric collections by name and click on the "Retail Stores" link on the left for a full list of retailers that carry their wonderful fabrics.

www.babylock.com and **www.tacony.com**

I was a Baby Lock fan even before they sent over their wonderful *Symphony* sewing machine. I was already the proud owner of a Baby Lock *Imagine* overlock serger and a Baby Lock *Coverstitch* machine. Every item in this book was sewn using one or more of these machines.

www.fairfieldworld.com

Check out this website for a wide array of quilt battings, including the wonderful *Fusi-Boo* that we used on the *Harlequin Quilt* (page 50). They also carry a huge selection of pillow forms.

www.thefabricfairy.com

A great source for imported, rare and hard-to-find knit fabrics. All of the fabrics seen in this book that are not my own or other Michael Miller prints came from *The Fabric Fairy*.

www.dritz.com and **www.brewersewing.com**

Great supplier of sewing trims and notions, including all the elastics and stretch trims used in this book's samples.

www.etsy.com

Not only a fabulous marketplace for handmade goodies but a never-ending source of all the materials you could ever need to make your handmade goodies! If you haven't checked it out yet,

Index